Mac M^c alister
Mary M^c alister

Cruising Through Life

Robert M. McAlister

Photography by Mary McAlister

ROCINANTE off the Brittany coast, 1991

ISBN **0-9748378-0-6**

Address inquiries to:
Robert M. McAlister
80 Bamboo loop, #172
Georgetown, SC 29440
mary.mac@gte.net

Published by:
Ross Editorial
228 Black Rock Mtn Ln
Independence, VA 24348
ross@ls.net

Printed and bound in Taiwan by Printing Asia

Cruising Through Life

Contents

Preface

We four sailors relax below deck, sipping red wine and listening to our old friend's sea stories. He recounts his first North Atlantic crossings as a seaman on a Corvette in the Canadian Navy in 1939, escorting convoys of freighters through the dangers of German submarines to northern Scotland. When he was in his fifties and his wife 20 years younger, they moved aboard their sailboat and have made it their only home for 22 years. They've cruised in Labrador, Newfoundland and Finland, have made several transatlantic crossings by the northern route and have wintered in Holland, Ireland,Cornwall, Spain and other foreign lands. Now, at age 79, he has reluctantly put their sailboat up for sale, but they won't be living ashore. They bought a share in our canal barge and joined us in France by crewing across the Atlantic on a friend's sailboat. They'll cruise the canals of France until November, when they'll join another friend's sailboat in Panama and cross the Pacific to New Zealand.

They're among the many fascinating friends and like-minded vagabonds we've met during 25 years of cruising. It's amazing to me that we were ever so lucky as to find this satisfying kind of life. I thank all of those individuals, mentioned and not mentioned, who made this account possible. I especially credit my wife, Mary, who not only recorded all of our adventures with photographs but also enthusiastically completed at least half of all the work involved in every cruise we took.

Chapter 1

How and Why We Made Our First Cruise

I'm lying awake in a forward bunk at five a.m., thinking of things I may have forgotten and things I haven't had time to do. I want to get up and get started but don't want to wake the others. My wife, Mary is beside me. The boys, Robert 11, Jamie 9 and Charlie 6 are asleep in the cluttered main cabin. Today, Sunday, Valentines Day, ready or not, we're leaving Belle Isle Marina, Georgetown, South Carolina, and heading south, down the Intracoastal Waterway toward Florida and The Bahamas, and we don't intend to come back until the end of August. This is the day we've been working toward for six months, ever since the day we bought this old wooden sailboat and started putting her in shape to make our first ever cruise. It's still too early and cold to get up, so I pull the blanket up and think back to the events that led to this day.

Three years ago, in 1973 I was an engineer for a construction company, building hotels and condos along the South Carolina coast. A friend from Georgetown, South Carolina, asked me to help him develop Belle Isle, a plantation he owned on the Intracoastal Waterway—the ICW—south of Georgetown. It was a fascinating piece of land, 75 acres of 200-year-old live oak trees, azalea and camellia gardens planted almost a 100 years ago, a Civil War fort, lakes that had once been rice fields and a site for a marina. Times were good and it seemed like a golden opportunity to become an entrepreneur, live the American dream, possibly make a fortune. I started the development alone but eventually needed two partners, one of them the principal owner of the construction company. The project's success became an obsession, and Mary and I spent hundreds of hours planning and managing the development, hoping to be compensated in the end. We even sold our new house in Columbia and moved into the first completed Belle Isle condominium. Mary began teaching art in the school where our sons were students.

Things went smoothly until our proposed marina permit was held up for a whole year by an environmental dispute. During that same year, 1974, the Arab producers quadrupled the price of oil and the American economy slumped into recession. We had completed the first several million dollars of construction, but the completed condominiums weren't selling well enough to satisfy the bank. Our project was in big trouble.

In 1975, I was forced to give up my share of the partnership in return for being relieved of the debt. It seemed unfair that three years of hard work had left us with nothing but a mortgaged condominium and some small savings from the sale of the Columbia house. I had a wife and three small children, no job, and bitter feelings of disappointment and failure. I questioned my future and wondered whether all of our working and moving around for the last fifteen years was worth anything.

Mary and I spent a lot of time discussing what to do next. We agreed that it was time for some big change, an adventure that would bring our family closer together and show us that we could accomplish something by ourselves. We decided to use our savings to buy a sailboat and escape "The System" on a long family cruise.

We looked at many boats along the coast of the Carolinas and finally found a thirty year old double ended wooden ketch for sale at a marina in Southport, N.C. She was a classic Atkins Ingrid, 38 feet long, plus a six foot bowsprit. She had no engine and the decks leaked, but she had enough room for five people and was beautiful to us. We bought her for $11,000 and named her MATRIARCH. I began to make repairs—including recaulking the entire deck, twelve hundred feet of raking out, cleaning, pounding in cotton, taping and squirting new sealant. A replacement gasoline engine finally arrived from Michigan but was the wrong size to fit the transmission. There were so many problems and delays I decided to have the boat towed back to Georgetown and have a new diesel engine installed.

Early on New Years Eve, 1975, Mary's father drove to Southport with me and my eleven year old son, Robert. I'd arranged for a local fishing boat to meet us at MATRIARCH'S slip. The fisherman, a tall elderly man with thick glasses and two hearing aids, showed up in a dilapidated rust-streaked wooden boat, smaller than MATRIARCH. She was a Harkers Island work boat, with the cabin forward and a rounded stern. Her wooden decks were stained almost black from fish oil we could smell ten feet away. The fisherman passed a hawser to me, saying he would run all day until dark, would contact the bridges by radio and give us hand signals when necessary. He told us not to bother trying to talk to him because his hearing aid batteries were shot. He walked forward to his cabin, started a powerful sounding engine and began to take up slack in the hawser. I was steering with the tiller and, as our speed picked up, found it difficult to keep from slewing back and forth behind the towboat. We were up to six knots when Robert yelled from below that water was pouring in through a pipe at the stern. I jumped up, took a step backward and fell through the missing deck hatch into the empty engine compartment—a cover for the hole was still being built. I scrambled to get up, as MATRIARCH headed for a mud bank. I yelled for Robert to plug the hole with anything he could find, at the same time throwing myself against the tiller to steer back into the channel. Robert stuffed a rag in the hole, then found a broomstick and jammed it around the rag. The leak slowed to a trickle and Robert began to pump out the bilge, which was now above the cabin floorboards. I frantically signalled for the fisherman to slow down but, if he saw the signals at all, he must have misinterpreted them, because he sped up. MATRIARCH squatted down in the stern as she exceeded her hull speed and water began to squirt up from the pipes draining the cockpit. I yelled for the rest of the broomstick and a saw. Robert pounded pieces of the broom into the cockpit drains.

Things seemed to be settling down when, all at once, there was a tremendous bump and MATRIARCH rode up 6 inches and stopped. The shallow draft fishing boat continued to pull, popping the hawser like a noodle. The fisherman said he didn't know MATRIARCH drew 6 feet and complained that the charts didn't show any shallow spots like this. The tide continued to fall as we ate lunch. MATRIARCH'S deck began to lay over, but by four that afternoon she was afloat and we were underway again. The fisherman said he hadn't known Georgetown was a hundred miles from Southport and that it would take two days instead of one. Before dark we approached a drawbridge, continuing at full speed ahead. The fishing boat could pass under the closed bridge but MATRIARCH'S masts would snap off like matchsticks. Just before we reached the bridge it swung open and we passed through. The fisherman looked back, grinning and giving the Richard Nixon V for victory signal.

It was after dark when we reached Little River to tie up for the night. The fisherman was using his spotlight to find the pier. When he spotted it, he slowed to an idle, but a swift current continued to push us along at high speed.

There didn't seem to be much room at the dock between the other boats, so the fisherman yelled for us to drop an anchor. By the time we dropped our undersized anchor, we were on the other side of the river, still dragging. The fisherman came alongside and handed us the end of another, longer towing line. He planned to fasten his boat to the dock and winch MATRIARCH across the river. Just as he tied his boat to the pier and the pull of the winch strained the line to the water's surface, I heard the sound of an outboard motor approaching from upstream. I saw running lights on the mast of a sailboat headed for the tight rope. The fisherman was blowing his horn and blinking his lights as, cringing, I watched the boat run over the line. Its outboard motor flipped up, revved and died. The rope spronged as it cleared the sailboat. Much yelling and cursing issued from the sailboat as it continued to drift downstream and out of sight. By this time MATRIARCH was almost across the river, picking up speed, with the long bowsprit headed for the piles and dock timbers. Miraculously, the bowsprit passed between two piles where the timbers were missing and the whole boat wedged there for the night.

Up the hill we saw dim red lights on a sign, ALL AMERICAN CAFE. Inside, a juke box blared honky tonk music and a few customers shuffled around, smoking and drinking beer. The bartendress told us there's no food, no other restaurant and no motel within five miles. We walked back to our boats, ate the rest of our crackers and Moon Pies and lay down to shiver and sleep, as the temperature dropped toward freezing. Next morning before daylight the old fisherman was pounding on the side of MATRIARCH, ready to get underway. We slipped on the ice-covered rotten dock boards as we pushed MATRIARCH out from between the pilings. Full speed ahead, we passed under two more drawbridges and a railroad bridge that stayed open all of the time, except for the rare occasion when a train passed. Just as we were passing under the railroad bridge, bells rang, lights flashed, the bridge closed and a freight train rumbled across. By two in the afternoon we were tied up in a slip at Belle Isle Marina. The fisherman ate a big dinner Mary cooked and said he had to be on his way. It was almost dark but he said he would avoid the Intracoastal Waterway, take the ship channel and motor all night in the ocean back to Southport.

A few days later I borrowed a pickup truck and drove to Charleston to get the new diesel engine. During the next few weeks my more experienced helper and I installed it. Mary withdrew the boys from school and took their books with her. We rented the Belle Isle condominium to one of Mary's schoolteacher friends. There were a thousand other things for Mary and me to do, but by February MATRIARCH was almost ready for the big escape.

A knock on the side of the hull wakes me up. A little boy's face peers through a porthole. It's eight o'clock. We're all up, rushing around, trying to get ready to go. The boys are excited. Their school friends and parents climb all over MATRIARCH. I know the parents must think Mary and I are nuts. Finally, MATRIARCH lumbers into the ICW, headed south. Mary and I have sailed dinghies and small sailboats but nothing like this 15-ton behemoth with a six-foot draft.

MATRIARCH embarks

After two or three days of motoring and nights of anchoring, and after two or three groundings caused by straying out of the center of the channel, all of the gear has been stowed away and a routine established. Also, the weather is getting warmer and everyone is spending more time in the cockpit and less time below. Before March 1, we tie up for a month in a marina near Melbourne, Florida to complete the rigging and other work on an endless list.

Mary and I already feel this trip is going to be a success and just what we need to make a new start.

We begin to practice sailing before we leave Melbourne and, by the time we reach Miami, we've mastered the basic elements of raising and lowering the four sails. MATRIARCH has a very basic sail plan with a fairly large main with two reefs, a small jib, a boomed staysail and a mizzen. There are no sheet winches, only blocks and tackle. The halyard winches for the main and mizzen are open reels, whose gears and steel wire can eat careless fingers. The bowsprit has no pulpit—we have to crawl out on it to put up the jib. MATRIARCH is steered by a big barn door rudder behind a stout ash tiller. The anchor is raised by an ancient Navy 01 hand operated windlass with a long lever bar. For navigation we have good charts of the Bahamas, including Kline's detailed charts and sketches, a fixed compass and a hand bearing compass, a primitive depth sounder, a very old Ray Jeff radio direction finder and a VHF radio.

The interior accommodations are also basic. The galley has an old propane stove with an oven. Water is hand pumped to the galley sink and the lavatory. The refrigerator is useless unless plugged into power at a marina. We buy block ice whenever we can. A classic Wilcox Crittenden "Senior" marine toilet sits on a pedestal in the head with its long bronze and mahogany pump handle always at the ready. Mary and I sleep in the bow V-berth. The boys sleep in the main cabin on narrow berths. Charlie's is eleven inches wide, Jamie's a little wider, and Robert has the pilot berth above one seat.

MATRIARCH waits at anchor in Hurricane Hole, Biscayne Key for fair weather to cross the Gulf Stream to the Bahamas. All preparations have been made. All entertainments have been exhausted, including a weekend at Disney World and a drive through the Everglades. A cold front brings 20–25 knot winds and big waves to the Gulf Stream, just outside our snug little harbor. For the first time we feel anxious about putting our children at risk in an unfamiliar and possibly dangerous situation. Are we doing the right thing, embarking on an adventure like this, or is it a fantasy that isn't going to work in the real world?

When I telephone a secretary back home to check on things, she tells me that a big construction company I used to work for is trying to get in touch with me. I telephone them and am flattered to learn that they want to fly me up there to meet with the president of the company. Leaving the rest of the

Crossing the Gulf Stream with Mary at the helm

family at anchor, I dig out a wrinkled coat and tie from the back of the hanging locker, take a taxi to the airport and fly to Greenville. I'm a fish out of water, interviewing with grizzled construction bosses, good old boys from Alabama and South Georgia talking about building nuclear power plants. They look at my beard, dark tan and rumpled clothes like I'm from another planet. Finally, I'm ushered into a plush office on the top floor to meet the president. He thinks I'm on vacation and tells me about a beach house he owns but never has time to use. He's flabbergasted when I tell him he should take more time off. When I tell him I could only accept a job if it's located on the coast, he turns off entirely and says he'll be in touch if anything ever comes up. I know I'll never hear from him. I fly back to Florida.

Finally, early on a beautiful calm Easter Sunday morning we get underway for our first long passage, fifty five miles to Gun Cay in the Bahamas. It turns out to be a smooth and satisfying passage, motor sailing across the deep turquoise waters of the Gulf Stream. We're at anchor by mid-afternoon in the harbor of Gun Cay to clear Customs. I know we haven't been tested by The Sea's nastier moods but we've taken our first step and escaped without a hitch.

Chapter 2

Cruising the Bahamas

This morning I'm relaxing in the cockpit with my second cup of coffee, feeling the warm sun on my back and thinking I must be in the middle of a dream. Here we are, our family, cruising through The Bahamas. Six months ago I looked up the definition of "cruising" in a dictionary. It said, "Traveling without destination or purpose, to go wandering about."

I come from a long line of wanderers—Highland Scot savages and hard-scrabble Scots Irish, stalking stags and painting themselves blue before battle. When the English took our bleak lands from us, we emigrated to South Carolina and fought in the American Revolution, hoping for a better life in this new world. My family were dirt farmers, shifting westward every generation, from South Carolina to Alabama to Mississippi, looking for better land. My father was born in 1900 and raised in rural Mississippi, the son of a country lawyer and farmer. He never heard of cruising. He worked his way through college, married his childhood sweetheart and worked hard for 42 years, managing business for Southern Bell Telephone and Telegraph Company. I was the only child, born in North Carolina in 1934.

I grew up in the South, digging forts, playing war and moving from one city to another. My adolescent dreams centered around pitching baseballs and trying to impress the many girls I longed to kiss. When I graduated from Georgia Tech, I joined the Navy, not because the sea was in my blood, but to avoid being drafted into the Army. After boot camp, faced with the prospect of scrubbing decks for 2 years, I applied to Officer Candidate School, extending my enlistment a year to get into the Civil Engineers Corps. After graduating from Navy school in California, I applied for duty in any foreign country. The Navy sent me to Beaufort, South Carolina, to help build a Marine Air Base.

It was while I was living in the bachelor officers' quarters at the Marine base in 1957 that a friend invited me to spend a week of leave aboard his 35-foot 1938 Chris-Craft fishing boat. I listed my leave address as "c/o the JUANITA JANE, Panther Johnson's Marina, Georgetown." It was a typical stifling hot humid afternoon in August when I parked my little Bugeye Sprite at the end of the sandy washboard road to Panther's place. Panther was sitting outside in the shade, shirtless in a broken chair, drinking straight scotch out of a jelly glass. His flushed weather beaten face was turned to catch a little breeze from a slowly whirling fan in front of his marine railway. He was trading sea stories with a couple of other old reprobates, who owned or worked on boats strung out along the dock or tied up in the rusty tin boathouse. I stopped to listen to a good one about a drunken U.S. Senator misbehaving with the Madam of Sunset Lodge, Georgetown's world famous house of prostitution. Then I moved on down the dock to open up and throw my sea bag on board the JUANITA JANE, letting out smells of mildew and rotting wood. She had a forlorn romantic look—like something left over from the movie set of *Key Largo*. I could imagine Humphrey Bogart or Ernest Hemingway at the helm. The JAUNITA JANE was still fitted out with outriggers, a fight chair and a chrome plated mile ray spotlight big enough for a battleship, but she had definitely seen better days and hadn't been to sea in a long time.

Soon, my friend, McConnell, arrived with a big cooler of iced down Schlitz, and we began to plan our vacation—the highlight of which would hopefully be a series of moonlit river cruises with eager and beautiful young women, already lined up. During the day we'd sleep and prepare for the next night's cruise. Unfortunately, the first night's guests failed to show up and we had to drive to Pawleys Island, a beach resort 20 miles north and shanghai a crew of college girls from the old dance Pavilion, a rundown barn of a place where southern belles used to hang out to drink beer, dance the shag and get picked up. It was after 10 o'clock before the JUANITA JANE was underway, guided by our drunken captain, singing "What will we do there? What will we see there? What'll be the big surprise? There may be senoritas with dark and flashing eyes. Hey!" The college girls thought he was hilarious. He pretended to scan the muddy banks of the creek with the powerful mile ray, looking for wide-spaced, red eye reflections from big alligators. There was much giggling and popping of beer can tops. At a wide place in the creek, McConnell cut off the engine and we drifted, jumping off the roof, swimming around the boat and playing hanky-panky with the girls. All in all, the cruise was a success, even when our captain approached the dock at high speed and ordered the crew to jump off and tie her up. Dock pilings whizzed by, way too fast to jump, and we bounced off a few, before a sudden and final stop. "That's what I get for trusting the lines to a drunk", he disciplined me. The girls, declaring their love for us, the sea and the JUANITA JANE, drove away, looking forward to other romantic moonlight cruises. By the end of the week, I'd developed a distinct liking for this kind of cruising life.

I finished my Navy career without so much as one day at sea and, by the spring of 1960, I was reluctantly back in Georgetown, South Carolina, working as an engineer for the International Paper Company. I was renting a little house on the backside of Pawley's island, with pink asbestos siding and HMS PINAFORE hand lettered on a wooden sign. There was no ocean view, but it was the only kind of house I could afford. I didn't like the mill or Georgetown, but living at the beach made it bearable for a bachelor, at least for this summer.

One afternoon I ran up the steps and began to toss off the hot sweaty work clothes that forever stank of the paper mill. I took a shower and put on a decent pair of Bermuda shorts and a sportshirt—I had a date that night with someone who might turn out to be more interesting than the local Low Country girls. One of the managers at the paper mill had a niece from New York visiting their beach house for a week, and he'd asked me to meet her.

I drove back along the beach road and stopped behind one of the big houses, its whitewashed cypress siding faded and louvered shutters peeling. I'd been told the house was built about 1840 as a summer academy for children of aristocratic rice planters. All of the planters' properties became rundown after the Civil War, and many were sold to rich Yankees for vacation homes. I walked up the steps, knocked on the double screen door, and was let into a big room with a high beaded wood ceiling, cracked plaster walls and bleached cypress floors. Porches on all sides shaded and cooled the room. As I sat on a wicker sofa, waiting, a young woman stepped through a door at the other end and said, "Would you like a beer?"

Everything was perfect. Her name, Mary Shower, what could be better? An artist, living in New York. The accent, pure New York. And on top of that, she offered me a beer, right off. And she looked good. After dinner at a restaurant in Murrells Inlet, we walked along the beach, barefoot in the edge of the surf, a moon overhead, holding hands. We talked about what we wanted to do in the future. We had many interests in common—architecture, travel, music. I told her about my Navy leaves in Europe and Brazil and my hope to be assigned to build a paper mill in Oregon. She talked about her time in graduate school in Arizona, her job in New York City and trying to save money for a trip to Europe. We sat on the back steps of her uncle's house until 2 in the morning. I kissed her. We decided to go out again the next night. I had decided that this was the one.

Before the week was over, I'd proposed and she'd accepted. We decided to have a short engagement and be married in December. After a whirlwind 6-month romance, the "wedding of the decade" at the Georgetown Episcopal Church and a week's honeymoon, we returned to our beach house to find that the water pipes had frozen and burst. We began our new life together, fixing things, dreaming up plans, compromising and making things happen.

A few months after the wedding, International Paper Company decided not to build a mill in Oregon. Rather than being stuck in Georgetown indefinitely, I found a job as an engineer with an architecture firm and was assigned to a construction project in Wilmington, North Carolina. Mary found a job as society editor for the local newspaper. After a year, I was transferred to a project in Chapel Hill, North Carolina, and Mary worked as a technical illustrator for the new Research Triangle Institute. While living in Chapel Hill, we prefabricated a house in the barn behind us and assembled it on a lot we bought on the Creek at Pawleys Island. Mary named the house MARSHMELLOW. After a year in Chapel Hill, I took a new job with Turner Construction Company, a large building contractor in Boston. We lived in Norwell, 30 miles south of Boston, with me commuting to the city by bus. Our first son, Robert was born on November 18, 1964.

While living near the North River and Cape Cod Bay, I was persuaded by a commuter friend to buy half interest in my first boat. It was an old 18-foot cedar lapstrake open motorboat with a Palmer inboard gasoline engine. BOAT, as we named it, was fine for fishing and exploring, until I hit an unmarked rock in the middle of the North River, which all the locals seemed to know about. After that I spent most of my free time in Vinnie Lincoln's Boatyard, trying to fix the leak. Following a second season of fighting leaks, I gave my interest in BOAT back to my commuter friend.

After 3 years of commuting and cold winters, I accepted a job with a big industrial contractor in Greensboro, North Carolina. Our second son, Jamie, was born there on October 19, 1966. A year later, I was offered a better job with a smaller but growing contractor in Columbia, South Carolina, where Charlie was born on March 4, 1969. The family was complete, three boys and Erich, the German shepherd.

While we were living in Columbia, a friend invited me to join the local Sailing Club and persuaded me to buy his used Penguin, a 10-foot bathtub of a sailboat used in frostbite races on Lake Murray. Mary and I learned to handle the little boat and we participated in some of the races, but without particular success. We weren't fond of the highly competitive attitude of the racers, although we loved the sailing. We decided we'd rather have a boat we could use to explore and take the whole family on. Mary's first priority was that the boat have a head.

In preparation for owning a bigger boat, Mary and I signed up for a boating course given by the Coast Guard Auxiliary. The course ended with a written exam. I completed mine quickly and turned it in. Mary agonized over each question and was the last person in the room to turn in her paper, as I waited impatiently outside. I was sympathetic as she worried that she hadn't done well. During the final class, when the results were given out, I had passed the course but Mary had made the only perfect score.

In 1968, Mary's parents moved from Connecticut to Georgetown to retire. My father-in-law, who had always loved messing about with boats, found a 28-foot fiberglass houseboat for sale. We bought it together and named it the QUEEN MARY. It had enough room for the whole family, with a galley and a head, although it looked like a house trailer on a barge. Its 200 horsepower inboard-outboard gasoline engine would move it along at an amazing speed, planing at more than 20 miles an hour. Throttling ahead at less than a plane produced large wakes, which tended to rock other boats and anger their crews. Even Mary's mother, who was a dignified land person of almost 70 who couldn't swim, enjoyed day trips on the QUEEN MARY. One Sunday afternoon, still dressed in her church clothes, she put one foot aboard, hesitated too long as the boat drifted away from the pier and did a split—hat purse and all—into the filthy river just below a point of waste discharge from the steel and paper mills. I, the hero, jumped in and saved all but her pride.

The QUEEN MARY gave Mary and me opportunities to make longer cruises and learn some basics of navigation and seamanship. The boat wasn't meant for the open sea, but was perfect for exploring rivers along the Carolina coast. It's only weakness, other than its horrific consumption of gasoline, was a tendency for the outdrive to break when it ran over partly submerged paper mill logs. Twice, she had to be towed to a marine railway for expensive repairs.

"Mac, why are you staring? You haven't moved for an hour. If we're going to start for Nassau today, we better leave soon. The boys are getting restless."

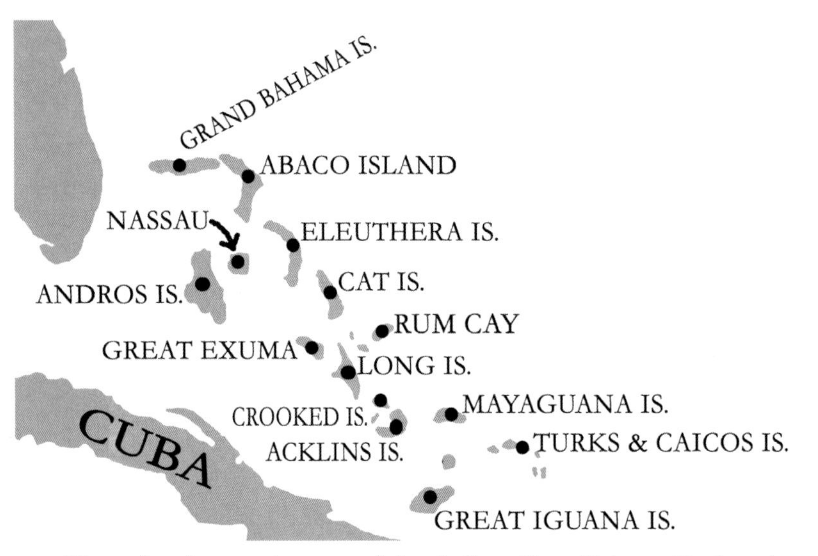

Three days later, we've crossed the shallow Great Bahama Bank and are nearing Nassau. New Providence Island is within sight but winds are light and we won't make it into Nassau harbor before dark. As night closes in, Mary and I squint through binoculars into the bright lights of the city, trying to pick out two green navigation lights that are supposed to mark the range of the entrance channel into the harbor. Automobile headlights and taillights move back and forth, making it impossible to tell what's what. I inch MATRIARCH closer and closer to shore, watching the depth sounder and the chart, which shows coral heads on both sides of the channel. After half an hour of looking, and almost deciding to anchor offshore for the night, we spot a faint flashing green light which doesn't seem to move like an automobile. When we head for it, we see the even fainter light of the other range behind it. The lights appear to be 25 watt bulbs on posts. We're in the harbor now but its impossible to pick out any piers or to tell if there are other boats near us. We turn out of the main entrance channel, drop the anchor and run our kerosene anchor light up the forestay, hoping for the best and turning in for the night.

View from MATRIARCH anchored in Nassau Harbor's turning basin

"Mom, there's big ships all around us." The boys wake us at daylight. There are three huge cruise ships looming over us, tied to their piers. We're anchored in the turning basin, blocking any of the ships that might want to get underway without running into us. We quickly raise the anchor and motor past Prince George Wharf and up the channel between Nassau and Paradise Island. A strong current is running against us but we finally pass under the Paradise Island bridge and turn into tiny Hurricane Hole Marina.

Leaving Nassau a week later, our family begins 3 months of exploring the Bahamas southward through almost all of the Exuma and Berry Islands. We learn from nature and from the people around us. We learn to work together to run the boat, to fix things that go wrong and to be a self-sufficient family. Each boy has his regular duty or chore. Robert and Jamie dive down to the sandy bottom and bring up live conch. Robert knocks a hole in the shell at the right place with a hammer and probes with a knife to cut the muscle holding the animal inside. Jamie shimmies to the top of a palm tree, knocks coconuts to the ground and prizes off the husks with a hammer and chisel. Charlie keeps MATRIARCH'S decks wet with buckets of sea water so they don't shrink and leak like a sieve, despite the new caulking. We meet other sailors and make many friends. We study lessons from books and collect objects from the islands and the sea. We fish and snorkel and prepare our own food, and live a primitive existence without suffering any hardship.

One midsummer day, MATRIARCH motors through Exuma Sound behind Staniel Cay and into a shallow narrow channel to the Happy People Marina. Like most of the other Bahama Out Islands, Staniel Cay is a low coral mass with mostly sparse vegetation and some beautiful sandy beaches with shells and coconut palms. The natives are descendants of slaves brought to the Bahamas over 200 years ago. The Happy People Marina is owned by the Rolle family, a common name on Staniel Cay. They also own the nearby Royal Entertainer Lounge.

The boys row their dinghy to another smaller island, just a lump of coral a quarter mile square and 40 feet high. At low tide they squeeze the dinghy under a rocky shelf and into the hollow interior of the islet, a dome as big as a house, with stalactites and pools of tropical sea life. A hole in the roof lets light into the interior. Later, to our horror, Jamie tells us how he climbed the outside of the coral and jumped into the cave pool from the hole in the top.

Mary and I visit the Royal Entertainer Lounge, a small block building with a concrete floor and corrugated asbestos roof, where Mrs. Rolle takes reservations and orders for the night's dinner, conch or grouper or hamburgers. The self-service bar is open all day, with a pencil and pad on the

Charlie's art in MATRIARCH'S cockpit

The boys show off their catch from MS. the dinghy

counter to run your own tab. The establishment is called the Royal Entertainer Lounge because Mr. Rolle had once taken Prince Phillip for a sail in his racing work boat, which had won the Out Island Regatta in Georgetown, Exumas more than once before it was retired. The rudder of that boat hangs on the wall with other artifacts. That evening we sit around one of the four or five tables for dinner. At the next table are four men, three Germans and a Bahamian from a sports fishing boat. They are enjoying themselves, drinking and telling jokes and sea stories. They take an interest in our family, especially the boys, now deeply tanned and with hair bleached almost white. One of the German men buys them ice cream. The Bahamian man leans across to Jamie and Robert and, with a serious face, advises them to value all chances to help their brothers. He tells them how lucky they are to have brothers and how much they will mean to each other in the future, even when they've grown up. Unexpected encounters like this, and the encouragement and kindnesses we receive all along the way, make the adventure even more meaningful.

We reach our furthest point south, Georgetown, Exumas. We motor sail across the shallow harbor to a point in front of the Peace and Plenty Hotel.

The boys and a playmate, Georgetown, Exuma

Jamie lets the anchor down and I shift the engine into reverse to set it. There is a crunch of machinery breaking and the propeller turns no more. I examine the transmission and discover a cracked metal casting. This town is big enough to have a telephone so we order a new part from Florida. There's a grocery store and some other diversions for the boys. There's an airport two miles out of town, where the part is supposed to arrive but doesn't. We learn to sail MATRIARCH without the engine, across the harbor to Stocking Island for a few days at the beach, and back again. The boys swim in the Peace and Plenty Hotel swimming pool, where Jamie saves a little red-headed girl from drowning. The girl's mother returns and takes her away without so much as thank you.

Day after day, I pedal our little fold-up bike to the airport, looking for the engine part on Mackey Airlines' one daily flight. Finally, it arrives. I clear it through Customs and pay the duty. I open the box, which is full of complicated machine parts, not the complete one piece transmission I ordered. There's no machine shop in Georgetown to put them together. Back to the telephone to reorder from Florida. No problem—it will be there soon. The complete transmission finally arrives and it fits.

MATRIARCH anchored off Stocking Island

Return of the conch snorkelers

We sail to the isolated island of Spanish Wells, where the natives are white fishermen. Their motorboats roar up and down the channel where MATRIARCH is anchored, and their motorbikes roar up and down the only road on the island. The boys swim with the pigs that are kept on a small

Jamie draws what he sees

island across the channel. We eat freshly caught crawfish in a purple restaurant. I order a cake for Mary's fortieth birthday from an old woman whose husband sits on a bench in the yard, mending nets.

We sail from Spanish Wells to Eleuthera, and through the tiny blasted-out entrance into a protected lake, the harbor of Hatchet Bay. The commercial harbor is busy with freight boats coming and going. The boys like to walk with sticks in their hands beside the huge chicken houses, banging the corrugated metal siding, stirring up thousands of flapping and squawking chickens, until they're told to stop. Charlie has made friends with Bahamian kids his age. They call from shore in the morning and Charlie skulls his dinghy to the beach to play. After hamburgers at the primitive Hatchet Bay Yacht Club, we watch an old movie, Seven Tall Women, on an outside screen provided by the Club. The harbor master, Mr. Albury, takes a liking to the boys and takes them fishing in his skiff. They watch him and learn to skin a grouper.

Anchored behind the lighthouse at Great Stirrup Cay in the Berry Islands, we watch a big white cruise ship anchor on the other side of the island. The passengers are ferried ashore in lighters to have a barbecue on the beach. Mary, the boys and I, all tanned and bleached like South Sea Island natives, stand in a palm grove observing fat white Americans eating and drinking. We're spied by a Midwestern couple, who think we're right out of the novel, *Swiss Family Robinson.* They ooh and ahh over our appearance and lifestyle. Others gather around, offering us food and drink. We walk back to MATRIARCH, feeling like we must be doing something really special.

We've learned to live a self-sufficient life without the comforts of ice, electricity and unlimited fresh water. We've learned to sail MATRIARCH long distances, to operate all of the gear and to navigate from one island to another. We hate to think of going back to civilization but we must. After two long overnight passages, we are back in the United States at Cape Canaveral, Florida.

Heading back home on the Intracoastal Waterway, we're anchored near Fernandina Beach when we decide to make one last ocean cruise, to Charleston. We get underway on a pleasant afternoon for the overnight passage. By nightfall the wind behind us is picking up and by midnight it's blowing 25 knots. Mary has sent the boys below. She spells me at the tiller, when a line on the staysail parts and I go forward to repair it. Suddenly a big

Great Stirrup Cay Lighthouse, Berry Islands

wave from behind tries to turn MATRIARCH sideways. The tiller whips across like a tree limb, knocking Mary sideways and almost over the side. She catches the coaming at the last second and pulls herself back into the cockpit. I run back and take the tiller. MATRIARCH has broached and is now heading into the wind, bouncing up and down with sails flapping wildly. I crawl to the base of the mast and try to pull the mainsail down to the first reef point but it's caught in the rigging and won't move. Robert and Jamie look out through the companionway hatch and are told to go back below. Charlie is still in his bunk seasick, as he's been from the beginning. Mary and I discuss what to do and finally decide to pick the best chance for a break between big waves to turn back downwind, toward Charleston.

We continue swooshing along at breakneck speed, riding the waves like a surfboard. By dawn I can see the size of the waves behind me, which is even more frightening. We're not sure where we are but, by dead reckoning, we guess we must be nearing Charleston. Between waves we barely see a red buoy in the distance. We sail close to it and identify it on the chart as only 10 miles south of the entrance to the Charleston ship channel. When we reach the Charleston entrance, it's still blowing hard. We must turn between the rock jetties at just the right time but, as MATRIARCH is starting the turn, a nuclear submarine looms out from behind the rocks, blocking the entire channel and causing us to miss the turn. We'll have to come about and start over again. I try to start the engine but it won't turn over at all. I'm exhausted and completely discouraged. I mention to Mary the possibility of calling the Coast Guard to tow us in. She looks at me like I'm crazy, declaring she won't allow the trip to end this way. She says we don't have enough head sail up to sail as close to the wind as we need to and suggests I put up the jib. I crawl out onto the plunging bowsprit and, with Robert's help, raise the jib. With all sails pulling, we sail straight up the channel in rain and lightning. The wind dies just as we're in front of the Charleston Coast Guard station and we anchor MATRIARCH there. Mary sets her camera up on top of the dinghy and takes the photograph that is on the cover of this book. The boys are excited and so hungry I have to take the dinghy in and find hamburgers at a fast food restaurant. On board, we celebrate MATRIARCH'S return and then crash for 12 hours. The next morning I check the engine oil and find it's full of sea water from waves which had come in through the exhaust pipe. I flush it out twice with clean oil, the engine starts and we motor back to Belle Isle.

By the time we return to Belle Isle, it's late August. We've made overnight passages, experienced bad weather and overcome many minor difficulties. Mary and I agree we were lucky to have been expelled from the rat race and given a chance to enjoy the most rewarding experience we've ever had. The kids agree they had the most wonderful time of their lives. They have plenty to tell their friends and have no problem advancing to their next grade. Mary has documented the entire trip with great photographs and has become interested in photography as an art form. I start my own small construction company, willing to take any job that comes along, and am successful in my business. Mary and I are confident that we and our boys have a bright future.

Chapter 3

A Temporary Return To Reality

Eight months later, one of my old construction bosses calls from Tennessee and asks if I have any interest in helping him open an international construction office in Athens, Greece. It would be a 2-year contract to live in Athens with the family, with all expenses paid by the company. The job would involve estimating construction costs for large projects in Saudi Arabia.

Mary and I talk it over and decide the opportunity is too unique to pass up. I accept the offer, turn my little construction business over to a friend, and we sell MATRIARCH to a couple from Connecticut. I make a trip to Greece to find a place to live, and rent a modest house in Kifissia, a cosmopolitan suburb in the hills above Athens. Mary, the boys and I fly to Europe in the summer of 1977.

My assignment in Greece involves sporadically working long hours for several weeks and then waiting, with little to do, for the results of project bids to come in. I play some tennis, umpire baseball games for the kids and coach an American football team of 11 year olds, which includes Jamie. Every Saturday morning during the fall football season, teams of each age group ride buses in full pads and helmets from Kifissia, along the crowded streets of Athens past amazed Greeks, to the NATO base to play games with the military kids' teams. Charlie, Jamie and Robert each play for a different team. The games take up the whole day and parents usually travel together to root for their kids and take advantage of a chance to buy American cheeseburgers and french fries at the base commissary.

During one of the games, the public address system interrupts with an announcement that I'm wanted on the telephone. It's my boss, an abrupt and demanding engineer, who tells me to catch the next flight from Athens to Frankfurt. The international air terminal is across from the NATO base, so Mary drives me there, I buy a ticket and get on the airplane without so much as a toothbrush. When I arrive in Frankfurt, I'm summoned to a telephone to learn I'm not needed in Frankfurt after all— but, since I'm already there, I'm to check into the Intercontinental Hotel and stay there until further orders. The $500 limit on my American Express card won't allow me to stay very long. Lonely in Frankfurt, Germany, I sit on a window sill in my hotel room, watching ice skaters practicing figure eights in the park. Later, I visit a department store and collect the clothes and other items I need to survive. When I try to check out, I'm told they don't accept American Express. I put it all back, go into another store that does accept AMEX and do it all over again. Two days later, after a brief meeting with a German contractor, I'm told to fly to London. After almost a week I'm back home in Kifissia. A few weeks later I'm standing on the ruins of an abandoned railroad bridge in a desert wadi near Tabuk, Saudi Arabia, feeling like Lawrence of Arabia. International contracting proves to be a demanding and sometimes exciting existence. While living in Kifissia, we spend most of our free time exploring Greece, the Greek Isles, Crete, Turkey, Yugoslavia, Italy, Austria, Egypt and Kenya. In 1979, at the end of my assignment in Greece, we move back to Charleston. I start a construction management business and buy a house in the Old Village of Mt. Pleasant.

Mary and I don't forget our love of sailing. For a year, we own a 28-foot cutter, ARIADNE, and sail on weekends in Charleston harbor. One Saturday morning in the summer, we and another couple get underway in ARIADNE for a 60-mile cruise in the ocean from Charleston to Belle Isle. Typical of the late summer, there's not enough wind to sail. When I start the engine, I notice that less than the normal amount of water is dribbling out of the exhaust, and the water temperature is going up. I go over the side to check for an obstruction in the water intake, but it's clear. Before I can discover what's causing the problem, there's a bang and clanking noises from the engine and I quickly shut it down. We sail on in light winds through the afternoon and into the night under a starry sky, toward Georgetown. We can see the white flashes of the lighthouse. As we approach the entrance to Georgetown harbor, which is protected by long rock jetties on both sides, we're confused by several flashing red and green lights. We've been in and out of Georgetown harbor many times and have no charts or other navigational equipment on board. We approach the lights, arguing over which light is which, and head toward the flashing green light we sort of believe marks the outer end of the south jetty.

Suddenly, we hear a noise we don't want to hear, the sound of waves crashing against rocks. Uh oh, we're on the wrong side of the jetty. Just in time we make a ninety degree tack out to sea, realizing the green light is on the other side of the rocks. We sail to the end of the jetty and turn through the entrance. The tide is running out and we make painfully slow progress against the current. About midnight, abreast of the lighthouse and making no headway, we anchor. We call the Coast Guard station at Belle Isle and ask them to assure our children, who are staying at a condo at Belle Isle, that everything is all right. A few minutes later another friend calls on the radio from Belle Isle and says he has talked the Coast Guard into towing ARIADNE back. Thirty minutes later, with our friend riding triumphantly with them, a USCG cutter arrives, everyone dons life jackets and we're towed through calm moonlit Winyah Bay to the marina. The next day a mechanic and I look at the engine. Somehow, I had mistakenly closed the engine cooling water seacock, the engine had overheated and a valve spring had broken and was bouncing around. Luckily, the repair was inexpensive.

During this year, Mary has taught the boys to sail a Sunfish in front of our house on Charleston harbor and is also teaching a sunfish sailing school for ladies, called the Crab Bank Ladies Sailing Society. Among her students is the wife of an ex-Governor of South Carolina. Mary teaches the ladies that they can sail as well as any man and that yelling is not necessary—lessons she previously taught me.

I've decided we need a new dinghy and that I'll just whip one up in our garage. Through an ad in a magazine, I buy plans for an 8-foot oak-ribbed plywood dinghy. When I finish buying the materials, plus a table saw and other tools I don't have, I've already spent more than I would have paid for a new fiberglass dinghy. In addition, I have to run electric power to the garage and buy a heater so that I can work through the winter. It takes me all winter, deciding whether to build it upside down or right side up, setting up and measuring, sawing out ribs, screwing and gluing, soaking and bending, sanding and finishing, and a whole lot of trial and error before I finally complete it. Still, it's not quite right, requiring a little body putty work at the stem where the plywood doesn't pull together like it should. I have to believe this is my last venture in the boat building business, but I do take some pride in the fact that I built her, especially after the defects

KOUKOUVAYEA at Guana Cay, Abacos

are painted over and the name, KOUKOUVAYEA (Greek for owl), is lettered on her bows. Now, we need a bigger boat to go with my dinghy.

To satisfy my ever present longing for a bigger boat, we sell Marshmellow, our house on Pawley's Island, and trade up to a new 36-foot Cape Dory cutter. We name her ATHENA. We take advantage of the first long holiday weekend for a shakedown cruise from Charleston to Savannah and back. Mary, our three sons—now teenagers—and I get underway at dawn, heading out through Dynamite Hole into the ocean, hoping to make Beaufort before dark. Winds are light and we are still north of Beaufort in the late afternoon. I let Robert take the helm to sail through the wide entrance into St. Helena Sound, a huge body of mostly shallow water, at that time still uncluttered by vacation houses along its marshy shoreline. In the gathering dusk, ATHENA sails a beautiful beam reach between low barrier islands, but it is pitch dark by the time we reach the flashing markers of the ICW. The boys are eager to continue south in the ICW, insisting that if tugboats and barges can do it, we can too. Reluctantly Mary and I agree for them to motor slowly south, but insist we'll stop and anchor for the night the first time ATHENA bumps the bottom. The three of them accept the challenge, picking out lighted markers on the chart and scanning the shore with a spotlight. They motor through St. Helena Sound, Brickyard Creek, the Beaufort River signaling the swingbridge to open, across Port Royal Sound past Parris Island Marine Base, behind Hilton Head and Daufuskie Islands, approaching the barrier islands off Savannah, all without touching bottom. By 2 in the morning, we're passing Thunderbolt Marina and I insist we stop for the rest of the

Mary at the helm of ATHENA, Ocracoke Island

night. They agree on the condition we get underway again by 6 AM, to avoid paying the dockage fee they had motored all night to avoid. They set an alarm clock but, when it goes off and I look out through the companionway, there in the cockpit sits a box of a dozen doughnuts and a Savannah morning paper, compliments of Thunderbolt Marina. Since we will be paying dockage, we stay until noon, exploring the little town and eating lunch in the marina restaurant. The next day we reach Savannah, turn around and head for home. We anchor for the night behind an island in St. Helena Sound. On the last day of the long weekend, we get up early and motor through the calm deserted sound toward the ocean, hoping to sail back to Charleston before dark. Suddenly, from out of nowhere, a speedboat appears, planing toward us at full speed. What could this be, pirates? Just as the boat roars up alongside us, one of the two men slaps a magnetic sign on the side of his hull, "US Treasury Dept," the T-Men. They request that we stop and that all of our crew come out on deck. They look us over, decide we're a harmless family, and roar away. ATHENA has a beautiful sail back to Charleston and is tied up in her slip before dark.

We're becoming more serious about long distance cruising. Whenever we can, we take longer vacations with the boys, traveling to the North Carolina sounds and to the Bahamas. In the summer of 1984, Robert, his girlfriend and Jamie make the first leg of a Bahamas voyage by themselves on ATHENA, traveling down the ICW to West Palm Beach where they wait for us. Charlie, having a tendency to become seasick, stays home. Mary and I join the crew and sail overnight to Lucaya, Grand Bahama. The next day we sail to the Berry Islands, rest for a few hours and sail all night past Hole-in-the-Wall and up the coast of Great Abaco Island to Little Harbor, in the Abacos.

Little Harbor is the home of a family of artists who escaped from New England years ago, to begin their solitary existence away from society. We stay here a couple of days, exploring the island, enjoying the atmosphere of a bar made from parts of a wrecked boat and buying dolphin-shaped brass belt buckles cast by the sculptor's son. We sail further north, inside of Great Abaco Island to Harbourtown. Harbourtown is a great place for beach-combing, conch fritters and exploring Elbow Cay. Here, Mr. Malone, now an old man, still builds Abaco sailing dinghies entirely by hand, using no power tools. Next, we sail over to Man-O-War Cay and anchor in American Harbor.

Man-O-War Cay is different from the other islands, with narrow concrete roads for golf carts and motorbikes, three boat building yards, an all-white population and three fundamentalist churches. Many houses are owned by foreigners, mostly Americans, and a few are for sale. I'm fascinated by a picturesque little cottage named Pirates Den that's for sale. I'm told it was built 40 years ago in Naussau as a two story house, eventually dismantled and transported to Man-O-War on a barge and rebuilt as a one story cottage. It's owned by an American lady who has recently sailed away with her man friend. I don't think I'm seriously interested in buying the house, especially since Mary hasn't even seen the inside.

At the end of our vacation, we sail north from Manjack Cay toward Charleston, 400 miles away. Seventy-two hours later, we're back in the marina in Charleston. I continue to think about the little house at Man-O-

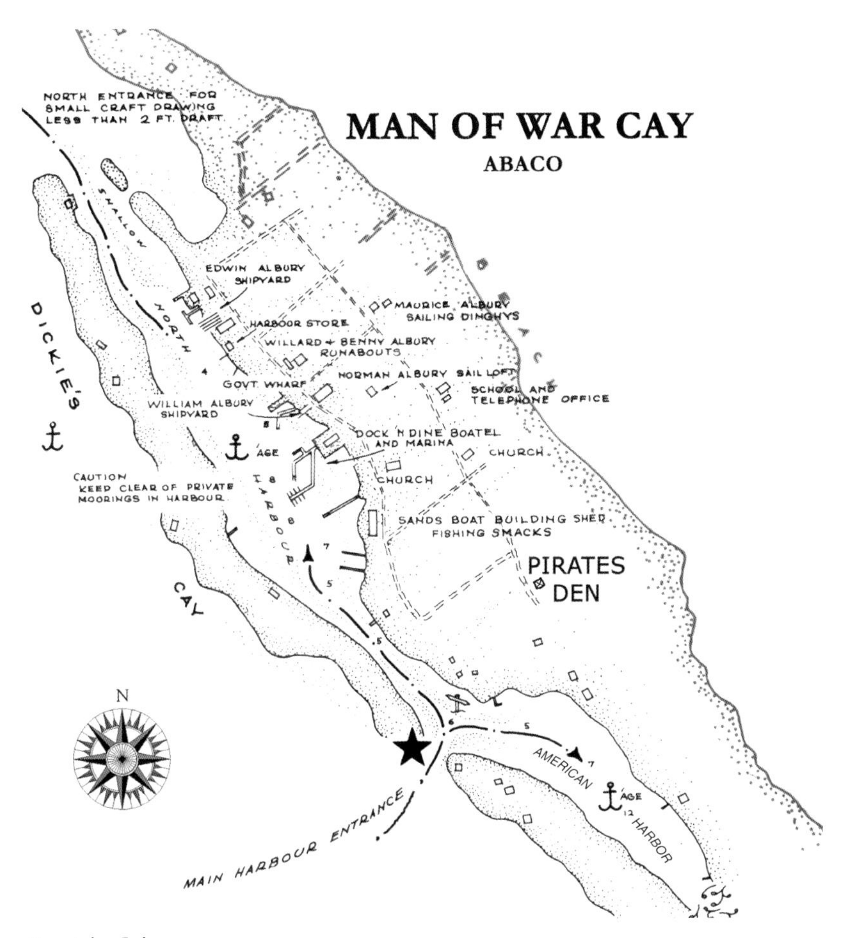

Our island home

War, perhaps the realization of a dream, a tropical paradise, coral sands, waving palm trees and my own sailboat moored at the bottom of the hill. I talk Mary and myself into believing we must buy it. I call the real estate agent, make an offer and contract to buy it. For a foreigner to buy any property in the Bahamas he must show evidence of "honesty and high character." I request letters of recommendation from our local police department, the minister of the Episcopal church, and a lawyer friend, which I send to the agent. Months later I receive a long involved document from an attorney in Nassau, the deed to Pirates Den.

Pirates Den, Man-O-War Cay

As soon as there's an opportunity, Mary and I take a week off to discover what we've bought. We drive to Palm Beach, leave the car at the airport and catch a little Cessna to Marsh Harbour. The Man-O-War natives run a ferry service to the Abaco islands. Any foreigner who owns property at Man-O-War is assigned a resident caretaker, who is paid a small amount by the property owner to look after the security of the house and to meet the owner at the dock with a golf cart and transport his baggage to the house. Harcourt and Vashti Thompson are the couple who look after Pirates Den and are also close neighbors. Mary and I find that everything down to the last knife and fork and all the linen go along with the purchase of the house. Nothing is missing for moving right in.

Pirates Den is located on a high ridge running along the center of the island, which is a narrow strip about 3 miles long. The south end of a concrete path, called the Queens Highway, ends in front of Pirates Den. The lot is small and there are other houses on three sides, but the tropical vegetation is thick enough for basic privacy. There are ten coconut palms and some sea grape, avocado and old fruit trees around the house. There is even an old fashioned bread oven, built of coral, in the back yard. The lot is not on the waterfront and the ocean can only be seen by climbing onto the wood shingle roof. The roofs of all of the houses are used to conduct rain water to gutters and into cisterns, which is the only source of water on the island. The house has a small cistern and an old fashioned hand pump for water to the bathroom and kitchen. There are porches on two sides for shade and wooden shutters that hinge up against the porch roof so you can open the house to catch the tropic breeze. There are two small bedrooms with a bath between. The rest of the house is living room and kitchen. When I look up, I see the underside of the hipped roof structure and the bottoms of the wood shingles. All of the floors and walls are Abaco pine. The windows are casement type, which open out. Most of the furniture is built in—much of it built by Harcourt Thompson, who is also a carpenter and house builder. There's a small iron Old Buddy wood burning stove in the living room, which must have come off some boat.

Everything—groceries, hardware, lumber, plumbing supplies—is available on Man-O-War for a price and is cheerfully delivered to our doorstep. The industrious natives, ancestors of English fleeing the United States after the Revolution, have been successful in turning their island into a bustling tourist haven and a center of commerce for all of the Abacos. They have become wealthy enough to build Florida-style houses, and they frequently fly to Florida for shopping and health care.

I soon realize that the American homeowners on Man-O-War must be wealthy enough to afford the high prices charged by the natives for food and home maintenance. To keep even as modest a house as Pirates Den, we'll have to do most of the work ourselves. We schedule family vacations to work on the house. One summer we build a platform on the roof so we can see the ocean. We replace most of the wood roof shingles, which are worn out from the hot sun, and install new gutters for the cistern. We build a mezzanine platform over the bedrooms for storage. We comb the beaches for driftwood to build furniture. We even attempt to dig a new cistern to supplement the original small one, but finally have to give up and hire a contractor to dig in the solid coral with a backhoe. We build coral rock walls around the property, using what's left over from the cistern excavation. The boys have become semi-skilled carpenters and plumbers. Mary and Charlie are house painters. We spend most mornings working and afternoons at the beach.

Chapter 4

Family Cruising in the Caribbean

By the end of 1986, Robert is working as a fisherman on a longliner in St. Croix in the U.S. Virgin Islands, Jamie is majoring in English at Wofford, a small liberal arts college in Spartanburg, South Carolina, and Charlie is finishing high school and has been accepted at the Chicago Art Institute. I'm doing pretty well renovating historic buildings and building new houses, but I'm 52 years old and becoming restless at the idea that I may never do anything else. Mary has just come back from an exciting 7-week trip to Europe with her father. She's raised three boys and knows they will move away soon, leaving her with an empty house and a burned out feeling. We both want another escape, like the one we had in 1976. Could we just quit for a year and go cruising in the Caribbean? How could anyone justify irresponsible acts that might jeopardize the security of their future? We consider all the reasons and decide to just do it anyway.

We look for a heavier duty sailboat, capable of rougher ocean sailing. We contact several brokers along the east coast, telling them what we're looking for. A broker in Maine has a 1984 38-foot Hans Christian cutter. It's a 35,000 pound, double-ended fiberglass boat, built in Taiwan, with a massive amount of teak trim, inside and out. She somewhat resembles MATRIARCH, the boat we sailed to the Bahamas in 1976, but is much more modern. Her intriguing name is ROCINANTE, the horse that carried Don Quixote on all of his misadventures. The broker tells me that the previous owner had bought her a year ago, his first big boat and the answer to his dream, that he and his wife would retire and cruise indefinitely. They had embarked on their maiden voyage up the ICW from Florida to Maine. When they reached Maine, his lifelong dream came to an end. His unhappy wife jumped ship and filed for divorce, and the boat is up for sale.

Mary and I buy ROCINANTE in March, 1987. The plan is for me to move aboard for a week to get her ready; then Mary and Robert will join me to sail her home. On a warm South Carolina day in late April I fly to Boston and rent a car. By the time I reach Kennebunkport it's snowing hard. The marina manager unlocks the boat and helps me plug in an electric heater. It's so cold

ROCINANTE'S tanbark sails

I crawl in a bunk with all of the blankets I can find and shiver myself to sleep. I wake up at daylight, still shivering. I push back the companionway hatch to see ROCINANTE covered in six inches of snow. I duck back inside. When I turn the water on in the lavatory to wash my face, I get a face full of antifreeze. Blinded and sputtering, I fill a pot with snow and melt it on the gas stove. Trying to wash the antifreeze out of my eyes and mouth, I splash water on the electric heater and short-circuit everything. Finally, I pull on all the clothes I brought, slip and slide up the frozen ramp to the car and drive to town to a warm cafe. The place is full of locals, joking about the late winter storm.

A cold rough passage, Point Judith-Norfolk, May, 1987

It finally warms up enough for me to begin figuring out what we've bought. The first thing I notice is how stable ROCINANTE is. When I shift my weight from one side to the other, she doesn't tilt an inch. She has a lot more gear than any boat we've ever owned. Two-speed, self-tailing winches made in New Zealand, a self-steering windvane and a life raft from England, a German diesel engine, a satellite navigation system manufactured in Japan and sails from Hong Kong. The bagged mainsail and genoa are so heavy I can barely drag them out of the forepeak onto the deck. They're a beautiful tanbark color and in good shape. Everything seems to work. ROCINANTE is only 4 years old.

I know the least about the Aries windvane, a complicated aluminum contraption that bolts onto the stern and is supposed to steer the boat by itself. I'm trying to attach it, when I drop a special stainless steel bolt over the side into 15 feet of water. The marina manager lends me a long-handled butterfly net and says to wait for low tide to dredge for it. Miraculously, it appears in the net after 10 minutes of dragging and retrieving all sorts of other metal objects from the muddy bottom.

After a week of running back and forth to chandleries in Portland and Bath, and a lot of trial and error, ROCINANTE is semi-ready for our maiden voyage, 1500 miles to Charleston. Robert and Mary arrive and we get underway the next day, out of the Kennebunk River and around Cape Ann to Scituate, south of Boston. It's a cold but easy first day, with light winds and everything working well. We visit in Scituate with our neighbors from 12 years earlier before departing for Cuttyhunk and Point Judith, Rhode Island. From there we have a 350-mile shot to Norfolk. For 3 days and nights we battle a combination of too much wind, not enough wind and winds from the wrong direction. We find out right away we need a canvas dodger at the companionway hatch. Cold wind and spray make standing watches at the helm miserable. Also, we need a cabin heater—there's no place to get warm. Somewhere off New Jersey, a huge basking shark, two thirds the length of ROCINANTE, surfaces and swims beside us, giving us the eye. Soon afterward, the wind picks up to 25 five knots and Robert has to go forward in a plunging seaway to double reef the main. We make pretty good time with just the staysail and double reefed main. We haven't yet learned to use the Aries windvane, and the electric autopilot consumes too much power, so we hand steer in 3-hour watches. I'll always remember staring down at the red glow of the compass at 2 in the morning, trying to concentrate on the course, nodding off to sleep and jerking awake in the cold wind. Finally, in a dense early morning fog, we pass close by the loud horn of the Cape Henry light and enter Norfolk harbor. Radar would be a nice thing to have, I think.

Jamie relieves me in Norfolk and I go back to work. A week later, at Morehead City, North Carolina, I relieve Mary. Robert, Jamie and I sail the last leg to Charleston. I stand the midnight watch as we sail past the Frying Pan Shoals light. We glide silently by the metal skeleton of the light structure, a giant spider outlined by a full moon rising out of the ocean. It's an easy 2-day passage to Charleston, with my sons doing most of the work.

Mary and I spend the summer and early fall trying to disconnect ourselves from routines and responsibilities built up over the last 8 years. At the same time, we're making final preparations, and loading ROCINANTE with a ton of food and supplies. There's an unbelievable array of stuff to be stowed away, including two folding bicycles, scuba diving equipment, a library of books and tapes, tools and spare parts and an entire Sunfish sailboat to be delivered to Mary's brother in Jacksonville. Mary, following advice from some article in a cruising magazine, tears the labels off several hundred cans of food, identifies their contents with a magic marker and stacks them in some order under the port berth. ROCINANTE lists three inches to port.

By November, 1987, ROCINANTE is as ready to go as she's going to get. Charlie has started art school in Chicago, Jamie is back in college and our house is rented. Mary and I have discussed whether to go down the ICW to Florida before crossing to the Bahamas or to go all of the way outside in the ocean. A salty old friend advises us to tack back and forth between the Gulf Stream and the shore, using no navigational instruments other than a thermometer in the toilet water, to tell when we reach the Gulf Stream, and binoculars to pick out the glow of Florida's east coast. With gales predicted and the stock market plunging, we say some hurried good-byes, bid farewell to all dangling loose ends, fill up the tanks with 200 gallons of water and 150 gallons of diesel fuel and motor into the ICW, headed south. We breathe sighs of relief and begin the "life that's but a dream, da-da-da-da, dee-da-da".

At West Palm Beach we cross the Gulf Stream to West End, Grand Bahama Isle, and clear Customs. Drawing six feet, we carefully pick our way through a maze of ugly yellow coral heads, crossing shallow Little Bahama Bank. Near the end of the day the depth sounder readings pick up and we relax in an anchorage behind Great Sail Cay. During the next 2 days, we round Great Abaco Cay to reach our destination, Man-O-War Cay. We wait for high tide to enter American Harbor and make ROCINANTE fast to a mooring below Pirates Den. We open up the house and stow our stuff away. I sit in a chair on the porch, feet on the rail, sipping a Mt. Gay rum. The sand in the yard has been raked in a pattern, like a Japanese garden. A hummingbird hovers at a red flower just beyond my bare feet. The breeze rustles the palm branches. I think, this must be what it's all about.

We wait for Robert, Jamie and Charlie to find their separate ways to Pirates Den for the Christmas holiday. I spend several night hours on Pirates Den's roof deck with a Reeds Almanac and a flashlight, identifying the brightest stars and trying to bring one down with my sextant to that part of the horizon not blocked by trees. I have a lot of trouble in the dark, noting the exact time of the starshot. Later, I painfully try to work out the calculations and look up the numbers in the HO 249, or whatever it is. When I plot my line of position, it shows I'm somewhere in Virginia. It's much more difficult here than in the celestial navigation class I took at the College of Charleston. I can imagine how the difficulty would be multiplied on the plunging deck of a sailboat.

The boys eventually arrive. We cut and decorate a casuarina pine branch for our Christmas tree. The presents are wrapped in old newspapers and tied with fishing line. With all of our reminiscences and celebrations, we've almost forgotten ROCINANTE. It's raining hard and a northeaster is blowing, when a woman in a yellow foul weather jacket runs up the hill from the harbor, calling out for the owner of the sailboat, ROCINANTE. She tells me ROCINANTE has chafed through her mooring lines and been blown across the harbor, barely missing several other boats, and is now pressed against the mangroves along the shore. Robert, Jamie and I run down the hill to the dinghy and motor to the side of ROCINANTE, where several sailors are already gathered, waiting to help. We manage to crank the engine and back away from the shore, but not as far as we'd like, because of the strong wind and the tangle of other moored boats. We let go the anchor and drift back, afloat but still too near the shore. There's nothing more we can do until the weather lets up.

Early next morning I'm on the dinghy dock peering through binoculars and seeing ROCINANTE'S mast tilted way over. She's hard aground and the tide won't be low for another 2 hours. I've checked the tide tables and the afternoon high tide won't be as high as the previous day's. I ride across the harbor in the dinghy, hoping to sneak by the other boats, but the crews are ready for me, popping out and offering conflicting advice about what to do. The general consensus is that I'll probably have to hire the island ferry boat to drag ROCINANTE into deep water with its powerful engine. Everyone is shaking their heads and offering condolences but I know they're thinking I'm getting what I deserve for not paying attention to my boat and not checking my mooring lines. I return to Pirates Den in a depressed mood, kicking myself and wondering what it's going to cost to hire the ferry.

I'm out there again 2 hours before high tide, measuring the depth of the water with a stick, now totally convinced there's no hope of floating off. I'm about to leave ROCINANTE to find the ferry captain, when Robert and

Jamie row up in a borrowed dinghy. They casually lower ROCINANTE'S 44 pound Bruce anchor into the bottom of the dinghy and row it out to the end of our 200 feet of chain. Ignoring my warning that the bottom is no good for holding, they drop the anchor overboard and Jamie dives down and digs it into a sandy spot. Back on ROCINANTE, they tighten the chain with the hand operated windlass and start to row away, telling me they're going fishing and will be back in an hour. I shout after them that it's no use trying to kedge off, the tide's not high enough and they'll break the windlass or the chain. Just at high tide they return, climb aboard ROCINANTE and put more strain on the chain with the windlass. ROCINANTE'S bow twists around and she slides out into deep water. They look at me and smile. I shrug and tell them I knew all the time they could do it. We tie ROCINANTE back to the same mooring, cover the lines with split hoses and rags to keep from chafing through again and return to Pirate's Den to resume our holiday celebration.

After the holiday, Jamie and Charlie return to their schools. Robert will sail with us from Man-O-War back to his job on the longliner fishing boat at St Croix. We're given a lot of advice by the American sailors and ex-sailors who own property at Man-O-War as to the best way to sail from Man-O-War to the Virgin Islands. Some say to wait until the end of a northeaster, then sail directly east for three days and turn right. Others say to take small hops down the Bahama chain, Dominican Republic and Puerto Rico, known as the thorny path. For a week we wait in vain for favorable winds following north-easters and finally settle for the thorny path. We wait an extra week at Pirates Den for a winter storm to calm down, then sail south through the Bahamas.

After a couple of pleasant stops in Eleuthera, we get underway from Governors Harbor early one morning, headed for Rum Cay, a distance of 150 miles. It's one of our first passages made in the silence of a favorable wind. By noon we've sailed through a narrow channel at Powell's Point and are entering 2-mile deep Exuma Sound. The wind has increased to 18 knots and we're making almost 7 knots with the main and largest jib. By sunset we're within sight of San Salvador to the east and Cat Island to the south. There's a quick rosy sunset, then absolute black. Robert is standing the first night watch.

The inside of the cabin is warm, cozy and quiet. It's difficult to move around because we're pitching in five-foot seas and heeled over at a twenty degree angle. Everything is well fastened down. The whistling kettle on the gimboled stove stays level and there's a feeling of comfort and safety in the red glow of the little lights below. I crawl up in the quarter berth, wedge myself between two bulkheads and listen to the pounding of the water against the outside of the hull. I can't sleep and really don't want to, until I know Robert has spotted the light on the south shore of Cat Island, at Hawks Nest. Our only means of navigation, other than bearings on shore lights, is the Magnavox satellite navigation system, which gives a fairly accurate readout of latitude and longitude about once every hour. It's a comfort when the SatNav beeps and the reading agrees with where I think we are and a panicky situation when it doesn't, or when there's no reading at all because the satellite is too low or too high on the horizon. About 2200 Robert spots the light, far away, and in the expected direction. Now, we're out of the lee of Cat Island, heading for the south end of Long Island, and nothing stops the Atlantic swells, rolling in all of the way from Africa.

At midnight it's my watch and I stick my head out of the companionway hatch into a different world, where night exaggerates sounds and feelings of motion. The wind, less than twenty knots, screams through the rigging and waves slam and pound against the hull. We pitch and heel, but never enough to put the rail in the water. Occasionally a slop of wave wash rises over the windward rail and drops down the back of my neck. After the first few minutes I get over my fear of black night and begin to pay attention to millions of stars and the bright planets overhead. I begin to enjoy a beautiful feeling of exhilaration, as water rushes past the hull at more than seven knots. About 0100 I spot the flashing light at the north end of Long Island. Leaving the wheel tended by the Aries windvane, I duck below to retrieve a hand-bearing compass and check our bearing on the light. At the course and speed we're maintaining, we'll pass a few miles east of Long Island and west of Conception Island, but we'll overrun our destination of Rum Cay before daylight. I ease the jib sheet, allowing the speed to drop below 6 knots.

Robert takes over again at 0300. At 0615 Mary and I are back on deck, looking at Rum Cay, dead ahead in the gray dawn. We hold off a few more minutes until we can pick out landmarks from the chart. A freight boat, the MAXINE, steams in ahead of us and anchors a half mile from shore. Robert and I drop ROCINANTE'S mainsail. Mary is at the helm, steering us slowly into the shallows, where we bounce off the only coral head within a quarter mile. Robert names the coral head "Mom's Rock". We drop anchor in 10 feet of clear water, close to a pink sandy beach.

Rum Cay was once a prosperous out island of the Bahamas, shipping salt, sisal and pineapples to Europe and Canada. Before 1900, the principal town supported more than 2000 people, descendants of slaves brought by the British to tend plantations more than 150 years ago. Now, 75 inhabitants hold on to the old way of life, farming a little, working for a diving resort down the beach or just hanging out at one of the two bars, enthusiastically banging checkers or spades and drinking a little rum all day. A few more young people move away to Nassau or Florida each year.

Paved streets with coral curbstones, shallow wells lined with coral blocks at each street corner, and abandoned stone houses with wood shingled roofs give evidence of a once prosperous community, now falling into ruin and being covered with scrubby growth that turns everything into wilderness. The old Anglican church, still used by an aging generation who remember better days, is architecturally identical to rural Episcopal churches in Low Country Carolina. A large graveyard along the beach is enclosed by coral walls but most of the markers are piles of long forgotten stones. It's a beautiful but hopeless island, destined for some archeologist's future dig.

The most hopeful present residents are cattle, let loose generations ago and now living wild on a relatively fertile island with sufficient water and no predators, except for an occasional island human, energetic enough to hunt and transport the meat to the table. Apparently these cattle continue to thrive and multiply.

Robert and I ride our fold-up bicycles across the island, along the rocky, bumpy, sandy road, past the abandoned two-story municipal building and jail, up the hill and toward the east beach, 3 miles away. As we round a bumpy bend, a lean white cow appears, facing us down, bringing us to a halt. We eye each other. We gather some throwing stones. He paws the ground. I advise that we should wait him out. The cow becomes bored, turns his back to us, and does a slew-footed shuffle down the road to a rock wall and turns right into the scrubby brush. We continue, relieved. A little further along, two more cows meander along the road in the same direction as us. We slow down to delay overtaking them. Finally, they hear us and turn to face us. It's

Anglican church, Rum Cay, Bahamas

a standoff. For the first time I look at their faces. They smile a strange lop-sided grin, reminding me of a mangy dog who once smiled at me in the same way. These cows seem amused by our little fold-up bikes. After a few more smiles, they move off the road so we can pass. We meet several more single cows and groups of cows, coming and going, before we finally crest the last hill and look out on a beautiful sandy beach. The steep slope stretches a mile in a crescent, with coral cliffs at each end. Sea oats and salt hay protect the shore against erosion and form a flat field that stretches back to the scrubby brush that covers most of the island.

As we start walking along the sand, I'm disappointed to see numerous footprints, unexpected for so remote a beach. Looking at the prints more closely, I'm fascinated that all of the feet are so short and wide. It's Robert who realizes that cows are making great use of this beach for one reason or another; probably to catch the sea breeze that drives away flies and mosquitoes. The high tide line contains the usual assortment of debris—pieces of wood, a kind of seaweed resembling kelp, a few small shells, bits of man-made plastic objects, and many glass bottles. The most unusual thing is that almost all of the glass has been broken. This is strange. It's evident that few people ever come here, and why would they want to break glass anyway.

As the afternoon wears on, we observe more cows, at first a few, then many, standing behind the dilapidated stone walls of the old plantation days. A few venture out into the open, grazing peacefully in the salt hay. By 1700, there must be over a hundred cows in view. Robert and I decide to hide out at the edge of the brush to see what's going to happen.

As the sun sets, all of the cows come into the field. Most of them face the sea, either catching the east breeze or looking out at something over the horizon. All at once, the moon rises in the east, three quarters full and very big and bright on the horizon. This seems to have a definite effect on all the cows, as they start along the beach, almost in a line, some snorting and pawing the sand. It's too dark to see any details, but I can definitely hear sounds of breaking glass, as the cows trample bottles and jars that have washed up on the beach.

A few minutes later, the planet Venus rises directly underneath the moon, a bright intense dot of light. Again, the effect on the cows is immediate. They slowly begin to circle the big field in a distinct line, counter-clockwise. The leader is a big white bull with widespread horns, snorting and bellowing. He begins a sort of slewfooted dance, which is copied exactly by all of the others in the line, even the little calves bringing up the rear. Just imagine a hundred cows dancing in a line. Faster and faster they shuffle, until the moon and Venus have risen high in the east. I know my ears must be deceiving me, but I could swear those cows are singing Shuffle Off To Buffalo in full harmony.

Now, as if a certain phenomenon has caused it, the line stops. Together, all of the cows walk toward the beach and lie down on their sides in the salt hay and, apparently, go to sleep. Robert and I sneak back to our bikes and begin the long trck back to the boat. The moon lights our way. We're too dumbstruck to discuss our amazing experience.

During the next week or two we make short hops and overnight passages to the Turks and Caicos Islands, across the Caicos Bank and on to Puerto Plata, Dominican Republic, where about fifteen southbound cruising sailboats are pinned down by a winter storm. A 40 knot wind is howling across

Caribbean (Turks and Caicos to Venezuela)

the reef and into the wide open harbor, slowly dragging our anchors through the deep mud of a soft bottom. For 2 nights we stand anchor watches, waking the others when we drag back too close to the freighter tied up to a pier behind us; then we pull on our foul weather gear, up anchor and relocate again. On the third night, Super Bowl Sunday, Robert pleads to go ashore, so I dinghy him toward the concrete pier. As waves bash the pier, he times an incoming swell and jumps off at the right moment. I back up and return to ROCINANTE. He has the handheld VHF and will call when he's had enough of Puerto Plata's nightlife. A while later, a couple from another sailboat row their dinghy over to ROCINANTE, bringing their tiny twelve volt TV. We sit below, bouncing up and down, drinking Dominican rum and watching parts of the fuzzy black and white football game. Their TV won't pick up the sound but our short-wave catches an out of sync commentary from Armed Forces Radio.

A few days later, when the weather's improved enough, we move on. We're sailing an overnight passage along the north coast of the Dominican Republic, toward the big bay at Samana. I'm enjoying the first night watch, alternately watching the moon rising on my left and the lights of a village in the hills to my right. First, I look at the village, then at the moon, then the village, then the moon. When I look back the next time, the village is gone. I panic. A freighter must be between us and the land. I make a wild turn to port. Still, the lights don't come back. Maybe my heading is off. I look for lights in other directions with no success. I finally figure out a power failure must have blacked out the whole town. I return to the original heading and find the moon in its proper place. False alarm.

A few minutes later I hear a VHF call from another boat, who says he's a half mile off our port side. The radio is in the cabin, so I turn on the Robertson autopilot and go below to answer his call. Robert and Mary are sound asleep. When I start to transmit on the VHF, ROCINANTE begins to turn to starboard, for no apparent reason. As I'm running back to the helm to get back on course, the other skipper radios that he's making a single-handed delivery to San Juan but doesn't have the chart he needs to plot his course. He wants me to plot his position and give him a course toward San Juan. I reset the autopilot, climb down the companionway steps and start to plot a course for him. I call him on the VHF but, here we go again, ROCINANTE turning toward the land. I run back up the steps, back to the helm. I hear him calling me again. I'd like to help but the VHF transmitter is affecting the control circuit of the autopilot. In the end he must have decided I don't know how to navigate. He says never mind, he'll contact someone else to get the information. I feel like a fool, but he should have had his own chart, anyway.

Samana Bay is easy to sail into, proves to be a pleasant place to visit, but is rough to get out of. We're beating into a stiff breeze on the nose with short steep seas. We bounce along for hours, making slow headway toward the wide entrance. We think we're having it rough until two tiny Dominican fishing boats cross our bow, flying sails the size of bed sheets, smiling and waving like it's just another pleasant day. Finally, we're able to turn onto a more comfortable heading, through the Mona Passage toward the southwest corner of Puerto Rico. We're back in U.S. territory, clearing Customs at the

Coast Guard base at Mayaguez. After a pleasant stop in Boqueron, we continue to beat our way east along the south coast of Puerto Rico and to the island of Vieques. During our overnight passage from Vieques to St. Croix, the U.S. Navy includes us in its war games. Bright red and orange lights blink and move back and forth near us, but without radar we can't tell what's going on. We tie up at Christensted marina next day and Robert leaves us to join the crew of his longliner fishing boat.

Chapter 5

South to Venezuela

Mary and I are alone again, still headed south but not sure how far we'll go before turning around. Originally we'd planned to go no further than Guadeloupe but now we think we'll go on to Venezuela. We've yet to experience a problem we haven't been able to solve.

It's the height of the Virgin Islands yachting season, with hundreds of sailboats plying back and forth, having fun. We see many elegant yachts with paid crews and millionaire charterers, one gigantic cocktail party. We get a kick out of listening on the VHF to Virgin Islands Radio broadcasting messages to charterers and inane conversations between yachts, arranging social activities. We steer away from the high-priced marinas and yacht clubs, anchoring out most of the time. Coral Bay at St. Johns is a laid back place we enjoy a lot. Many poor sailors are here, living beach bum lives. Jost van Dyke is nice. Gorda Sound has many anchorages and there is lots to do at Drakes, Bitter End, Tradewinds, Biras Creek and other resorts. We call home from the British Virgin Islands and find out Charlie has dropped out of the Chicago Art Institute—he doesn't like it. There's nothing we can do from here. Mary's 85-year-old father is on his way to St. Martin to join us. Jamie is to meet us in Grenada after school is out.

We don't have to beat to the east anymore, but boisterous March winds delay our overnight passage from Gorda Sound to St. Martin. When we arrive at Phillipsburg a day late, Mr. Shower, as I always address my father-in-law, is eager to move his suitcases out of the hotel and on board ROCINANTE. He's a retired Navy Reserve Commander and the man who first taught me to sail small boats. He's spry for his age and climbs in and out of our rubber dinghy without difficulty. We move out of the roly St. Phillipsburg anchorage and through a drawbridge into the supposedly more secure Simsons Lagoon anchorage. We plan to stay here awhile and visit the island of Saba by charter boat, but a combination of strong gusts of wind from the hills and reports of recent thefts from untended boats changes our minds. The next morning, in the face of a strong wind, we beat 30 miles to St. Barts. Mr. Shower stands wedged in our dodgerless companionway, soaked by spray, enjoying every minute of the trip. We anchor outside the crowded harbor at Gustavia. We spend the next week in this chic French environment, eating gourmet meals at Mr. Shower's expense and exploring the island in a rented Gergel jeep. At the end of the week, we watch in awe as little passenger planes dive down the face of the mountain to land on a very short runway, terminating in the surf. Mr. Shower flies back to his retirement village in Charleston.

Freight boat PERSERVERANCE II, Basseterre, St. Kitts

Improving weather allows us to anchor for 2 days in the open roadstead at St. Eustatious, a Dutch island dominated by an extinct volcano known as The Quill. The only town, Oranjestad, was a principal trading port of the Caribbean during the 18th century but is now a sparsely settled but interesting architectural relic of stone ruins and restored buildings. Our next destination, St. Kitts, is within sight of St. Eustatious. We cross over and anchor in the commercial harbor at Basseterre. Next to us is the PERSEVERANCE II, a battered wooden freight schooner from Trinidad. She's gaff rigged with two telephone pole thick, stubby masts. Her patched faded sails are wrapped around her wooden booms. Tarps cover her deck cargo as the crew patiently waits for docking space so they can unload. Her captain tells me she's the last of her kind.

We must clear Customs in an office above the Basseterre Post Office, where a bald little black man sits behind an enormous rolltop desk shuffling papers. Scowling over his gold-rimmed spectacles, he motions to us. He answers his telephone, talking low and chuckling for several minutes before, hanging up and shouting, "Who's next?" I stand in front of him. "Where are your papers?" I hand him ROCINANTE'S documentation form and exit papers from St. Eustatious. "Where are your crew lists?" I explain I have no forms for filling out the crew list. "No list" he repeats with a disgusted sneer. He pulls some forms from a cubby hole and shoves them in my direction. "Who's next?" As I fill out the crew lists, a freighter crewman stands at the desk. "Are you the captain? No? I always see the captain. The papers are not right. You cannot unload. Go back to Dominica. Next". I hand him the forms. He examines them. "Are you going anywhere else?" I tell him we're going to Nevis, an island I assume belongs to St. Kitts. He reaches in another cubby hole. "Fill these out, three copies. Next." I fill them out, wait in a lengthening line and hand him all of the papers. He slowly and painfully copies our names in a ledger. He looks up. "Thirty-three E.C. dollars." I hand him an E.C. fifty dollar bill. "I said thirty-three dollars. We do not make change. Go change it and come back." I make change at the grocery store across the street, but it's only after the Customs official's long lunch break that I finally get the stamped papers we need. I haven't had to deal with anyone like him before but I'm sure there will be others.

After St. Kitts and Nevis, we anchor for a night off Montserrat, an island with an active volcano and no good harbors. We sail on to the group of islands called Îles des Saintes, a dependency of Guadeloupe. There's no Customs office here, suggesting the more relaxed attitude of the French. After a few days at these pleasant islands, we arrive at the large crowded marina at Pointe-A-Pitre on the mainland of Guadeloupe. All of the boats are tied up, fore and aft to a long concrete pier with no finger piers. We spot one empty space. We're supposed to pick up a mooring buoy as we head for the pier, using it to hold our stern away from the other boats. Mary tries to fasten on to the floating ball with a boat hook but the ball disappears under ROCINANTE'S stern. Mary throws a line from the bow to a French sailor on the pier, who ties it off to a cleat and walks away. When I put ROCINANTE'S engine in reverse to stop us from running into the pier, a line

Bequia donkey, Grenadines

dangling from the mooring buoy wraps around the prop. We're caught 20 feet short of the pier with no way to move. I pull off my clothes and jump into the filthy marina water with a knife to cut the line away from the prop. Ten minutes later, we finally get rid of the line and pull the bow in, until the bowsprit overhangs the concrete pier. Clumsily, I jump down to the pier, check in at the marina office and am told that ROCINANTE is in someone else's slip, and we'll have to move to another slip. Taking pity, he assigns us an easier slip to get into.

We sail from Guadeloupe to Fort de France, Martinique, anchoring off a beach where topless tourists bake in the Caribbean sun. We continue down the line of islands to St. Lucia, first to the inner harbor of Rodney Bay, a paradise of Happy Hours, and then to the pocket sized harbor at Marigot Bay, jammed with cruising boats and tourists. Boat boys work the fleet, peddling palm thatched hats and local bananas. A day later, we're anchored in the harbor of Admiralty Bay, at the northernmost Grenadine island of Bequia, a less touristy but friendly place where 4000 black and white natives live together, farming, fishing and minding their own business. We're in front of the Frangipani Hotel, sharing their dinghy dock with many other cruising sailors. We enjoy our stay here, taking long walks across this sizable island,

TRADE WIND, Princess Margaret Bay, Bequia

which has enough rainfall to have wooded valleys and fertile fields. We rest on a grassy hilltop, looking down on magnificent beaches and the cerulean blue water of the Caribbean.

We particularly admire a little British sloop, TRADE WIND, anchored near us. We meet the owners, Phil and Jill from Cornwall, England, who have sailed their 26-foot, 50-year-old Harrison Butler sloop across the Atlantic during the past year and are going in our direction. We're becoming better acquainted, drinking a beer in a bar-restaurant-boatyard overlooking the harbor, when I notice through the window that ROCINANTE'S inflatable dinghy, RUBBER DONKEY, is caught under the dock, with the tide rising. Phil and I rush down to free it before it becomes permanently stuck or punctured. I'm lying upside down in the bottom of the dinghy, pushing up with my feet against the underside of the dock. Phil pulls and the dinghy finally pops loose. We rejoin the girls, finish our beers and prepare to pay the bill, when I discover my wallet is missing. Undoubtedly, it fell out of my little pocket while wrestling with the dinghy. It won't have sunk to the bottom, either, because I purposefully changed to the floating kind of wallet after my last experience of dropping one overboard. Now this one has floated away, full of credit cards and cash, into the hands of no telling whom. I spend the next few hours telephoning cancellations of cards and making arrangements for replacements.

While at Bequia, we book passage on the FRIENDSHIP ROSE, a freight boat that sails daily to St.Vincent. We share the deck with livestock, stacks of concrete blocks, and other passengers, as the crew hoists tattered sails to assist the old diesel engine. At St. Vincent, capital of the Grenadines and once an important British colony, we visit the Royal Botanical Garden where plants and trees were brought from all over the world by the likes of Captain Cook and Captain Bligh.

Reluctantly leaving Bequia, we make our way down the chain of Grenadines—Mustique, Canouan, Tobago, Mayreau, Petit St. Vincent, Palm Island and Carriacou—all beautiful and enchanting islands at the southern end of the Windwards. Here, there's always plenty of steady breeze, with little need for an engine except to get underway and to set the anchor.

Gusty night winds in the Grenadines
lay ROCINANTE hard back against her chain,
anchored in the crescent of Tyrell Bay,
encircled by the isle of Carriacou.

Scudding clouds are swept away.
A half moon and bright Venus silhouette
sailboat masts, dark mountain tops
and a shore lined with dim lights.

A dog barks, the only village sound.
Boats of poor fishermen dot the beach.
Orange lamps flicker in the hills
Where Rastas with their dreadlocks live.

From the west, red and green lights
mark a ship approaching shore.
A jutting bowsprit and two tall masts
of a schooner, skirting the fringing reef.

She glides in silence, close astern,
a black pirate from another time.
Shouts in French, they let her anchor go.
Chain rattles, clanks slowly and all is quiet.

Now, behind her, a single piston throbs,
slowly thumps a mournful beat.
A Dutch double ended ketch
Creeps in, mizzen flogging, to a stop.

Her engine's down, her lights are out.
All is quiet now, except for
halyard slaps on wooden masts
and from the hills a rooster's crow.

Siren behind palm tree, Sandy Cay, Grenadines

We anchor for a night off tiny palm fringed Sandy Cay. Just at daybreak, two open dories of fishermen row close by ROCINANTE. A swimmer leads the boats, trying to find schools of fish, so they can surround them with their nets. The captain shouts, "Is coffee ready?" I wave. They smile and pass by. From Sandy Island we sail into the harbor at St. Georges, Grenada. The marina is still strewn with sunken boats from President Reagan's attack to rid the island of communism. Jamie arrives on June 4, landing at the big airstrip the Cubans built a few years ago. We celebrate with a fourteen course dinner at Mamas Restaurant featuring armadillo, possum and red land crabs served by the imposing owner, wearing her New York Yankees baseball cap. We apply for and pick up our visas for entering Venezuela. In company with TRADE WIND, ROCINANTE sails from Prickly Bay, Grenada, overnight to the wild Venezuelan islands of Testigos. Next day we sail into an anchorage off Porlamar, a city of tourist hotels on the big island of Margarita. After a week of exploring Margarita, we sail to Cumana, on the mainland of South America, and tie up at the marina.

Everything is taken care of at Cumana Marina by Mr. Bolivar, who arrives every morning to tend the needs of foreign sailors. For a fee he steers us through Customs, exchanges money, finds spare parts and arranges for laundry. This is a wonderful place, with Polar beer three dollars a case, rum two dollars a liter and diesel fuel twenty cents a gallon. Many sailors leave their boats at Cumana Marina to explore the country, as we do. We fly to Caracas, then Barinas, where we rent a jeep and drive up, ten thousand feet above sea level, into the Andes mountains.

Our destination is the Los Frailes Hotel, built in 1640 as a monastery. The setting is lovely, and it is dramatically cooler here. We're enveloped in clouds, and water drips from everything. We sit in the hotel bar, sipping hot cocoa with rum and cinnamon, listening to classical music and looking out of the open windows. Flowers bloom in green fields and water roars past in rocky streams. Horses and llamas graze on a hill. This is a paradise. After 2 nights, we drive higher into the mountains, to Merida, to ride the Teleferico, a 7 mile long cable stretching up the mountain to an elevation of 15,000 feet. We sail up between the snow-covered peaks of Mt. Bolivar and Mt. Humboldt, hundreds of feet above the sloping rock, gliding and swinging in little hanging buses.

Canaima, Venezuela, below Angel Falls

We fly back to Caracas, waiting for another Avensa Airline flight to Canaima. This flight lands in a jungle resort along a roaring tributary of the huge Orinoco River. We've come to see Angel Falls, the longest free fall of water in the world, named after a Missouri bush pilot, Johnny Angel, who, with his wife, landed his plane on top of a flat topped tupoy mountain in the 1930's and climbed down to safety. We make several day trips, including an exciting body-soaking walk across a ledge under a roaring waterfall, an Indian led log canoe trip down the rapids, a long hike through the jungle to the base of Angel Falls and a small plane flight to Angel Falls canyon and over the mountain. We stay an extra day because our Avensa airplane has a mechanical problem. When we do take off, the Avensa pilot announces the special bonus of flying into the canyon to view the falls. He describes the view as the vertical rock cliff looms closer and closer, then all is quiet in the cockpit, there is the sudden sound of straining engines trying to climb over the mountain and finally, a burst of applause when the plane barely clears the top.

ROCINANTE leaves Cumana on July 5 for St Croix, less than a 4-day sail. I'm in a hurry to get back home before the height of hurricane season. When we arrive in Christensted, Robert has just returned from a week-long fishing trip and we watch him and the rest of the crew unload 8000 pounds of big swordfish and tuna. They're weighed, packed in ice-filled containers and flown to market in the United States. Robert and Jamie have a big reunion celebration and are so hung over they are almost useless the morning we leave for Man-O-War Cay, 850 miles away. In addition, unbeknownst to me, Robert had fallen off his bicycle the day before and may have broken a shoulder bone. Going is slow, with very little wind and a lot of oppressive heat. We have to motor most of the time to make any headway. In addition, the Sat Nav blows a fuse after the first day and we have no means of navigation other than dead reckoning, sextant sun shots and an occasional fix from passing freighters. I have trouble with noon sextant sunshots, because the sun is almost directly overhead this close to the Equator, and because I'm so rusty at using the sextant and making the calculations.

Robert and Jamie on the passage from St. Croix to Man-O-War

There are some weather forecasts of possible tropical disturbances but nothing materializes. We troll most of the time but catch nothing. We stick to a routine of watches and chores, mostly steering by autopilot. Our hot tired little BMW diesel drags the dirty and overloaded ROCINANTE through thick oily swells. Finally, on the sixth night, we spot the flashing glow of Elbow Cay light, ahead. The next day we tie up to clear Customs at

Marsh Harbor, Abaco, Bahamas. Robert, whose arm has been tied to his side for a week, catches a flight back to St. Croix to resume work.

ROCINANTE on the marine railway, Man-O-War

We motor across to Man-O-War, waiting for high tide so ROCINANTE'S 6-foot draft can clear the shallow entrance. We move into Pirates Den and settle down. Robert calls to say his shoulder is in a cast but he'll be OK soon. We arrange for ROCINANTE to be pulled out on the marine railway at Edwins Boatyard, so the bottom can be painted. She looks salty and regal with her bowsprit overhanging the Queens Highway. Her bottom is painted with the very inexpensive paint we bought in Venezuela.

ROCINANTE is back on a mooring in American Harbor, and we have become so lazy we don't want to leave to go home. It's August 23 before we get underway. About 2200 of the first night we're still off the coast of the northern Bahamas when Mary thinks she sees a boat with no lights, far behind us. She calls Jamie and me, and we confirm that it's definitely a boat and getting closer. I don't know why it has no navigation lights and I don't like the possibility of it being a drug runner or pirate, out to rob or take our boat. We call on the VHF but there's no answer. The boat is only a few hundred yards off our stern and I can see a top hamper of antennas silhouetted against the starry sky. The boat is much bigger than ROCINANTE and is now holding course and speed to stay about a hundred yards behind us. Suddenly, it increases speed, roars up to within a hundred feet of us and flashes a powerful spotlight on our stern. Ten seconds later it turns ninety degrees to port, revealing the orange stripe of the U.S. Coast Guard, and speeds away. We're a little pissed at their behavior but relieved to know who it was.

The wind is steady from the southeast and, with help from the Gulf Stream, we're making 9 knots toward Charleston. Sixty-one hours after leaving Man-O-War, we're back in our permanent marina slip. It's our fastest passage of the trip.

Chapter 6

Crossing the Atlantic

I already know we've become too spoiled by the Caribbean trip to settle down forever. I now realize how lucky I am to have a partner who is gutsy enough to undertake almost any voyage I dream up. I don't think there are too many like her. This time next spring we're planning to sell our house and make a 2 or 3 year cruise across the Atlantic to Europe. ROCINANTE sits ready in Wild Dunes Marina at Isle of Palms. A hurricane is threatening the east coast. I've been out of town for 2 days and, when I return, Hurricane Hugo is too close for me to do anything more to ROCINANTE than double up the lines, strip off the sails and hope for the best. She's tied up, along with 150 other boats, to floating piers in a protected basin a half mile back from the ocean front.

The white-bearded owner of a Swan sloop across the pier from ROCINANTE tells me he's going to stay on board his boat, storm or no storm. He'd crossed the Atlantic alone 2 weeks ago, has no home except his boat and no insurance for his boat. He'd been trying to get some insurance coverage, but it's too late now. The trawler owner near us tells him no one can stay on their boats or on the island because the police have ordered evacuation of the whole island. He offers to put the sailor up at his house in Florence, 80 miles inland. They argue until the sailor finally agrees to go with the owner of the trawler. The sad old sailor comes up from below and hands me a mahogany box containing his sextant and some books to keep for him until he returns after the storm.

Hurricane Hugo hits us dead center during the night of September 20, 1989, with 130 mile an hour winds and a storm surge 15 feet above normal. Our house is damaged, along with most other buildings within 40 miles of Charleston. The only bridge to the Isle of Palms has been blown over into the ICW. Two days after the hurricane Jamie and I launch our inflatable dinghy and motor 5 miles up the ICW to what used to be Wild Dunes Marina. The marina basin is an empty lake. All of the boats and floating piers are gone, lifted by the storm surge and blown across the ICW onto the shore of Goat Island, where they lie in a tangled confusion of metal and fiberglass. It takes half an hour to find the battered ROCINANTE, lying on the bottom of the pile, pushed down into the mud by other boats on top of her. She's still tied to her pier. The Swan with no insurance lies beneath ROCINANTE'S bowsprit.

ROCINANTE on Goat Island after Hurricane Hugo, 1989

The Goat Island Yacht Club has been chartered, with membership restricted to owners of boats washed up on the island. The first meeting is at our house and is attended by boat owners and insurance company representatives. A salvage company is selected. A few weeks later a big barge with a crane arrives at the scene and boats are lifted, one at a time off the pile. Those that are intact are towed to the marina; the others are stored on another barge. ROCINANTE is the next to last to be lifted. She floats, has no holes in her hull and her engine runs. An insurance adjuster makes a list of her considerable amount of cosmetic damage, including bent stainless steel and bronze, splintered teak boards, gouged fiberglass and a broken windvane and other equipment. There's a shortage of local talent to repair the many badly damaged boats and most of them have to be taken elsewhere for repair. The owner of the Swan returns to retrieve his sextant and tells me he's got at least a year of repairs to make but he'll live aboard his boat in a boatyard near Wilmington while he does the work himself.

ROCINANTE, next to last to be lifted off Goat Island

My construction business is inundated with pleas from owners of damaged buildings to make cost estimates and repair damage, and I'm too busy to give much thought to ROCINANTE. Robert returns from St. Croix and Charlie from Chicago to help. Robert and a friend motor ROCINANTE down the ICW to Ft. Lauderdale, to the Hans Christian dealer who originally commissioned her. He has agreed to manage her repairs. However, by the time ROCINANTE arrives, he and his wife have had a fight, and he's getting ready to leave permanently on his motorcycle for the West Coast. He has transferred the responsibility for ROCINANTE'S repairs to another Hans Christian owner, a Brazilian man, newly arrived in Florida, who admits that he knows not a lot about boat repair. The insurance company has finally and reluctantly agreed to a repair settlement of $75,000.00, an enormous sum which our Brazilian believes will be more than enough to make the repairs.

Our English friends, Phil and Jill on TRADE WIND, had sailed to Maine during the summer and, after Hugo are returning to Charleston to visit and help us. On the way down the ICW, they meet another British couple on a beautiful 35-foot cold molded wooden yawl, who agree to sell her to our friends. Phil and Jill had previously been offered an acceptable price for the 26-foot TRADE WIND, and the deals are consummated at our house. The new owners of TRADE WIND, an eccentric heiress and her Rasta Antiguan musician boyfriend, arrive at our house to take possession of their new boat, as our Charlestonian neighbors peek out of their curtained windows in horror. Phil and Jill move aboard their new boat, DELIVERANCE. At Christmas the worst snowstorm in Charleston's history arrives and makes life on DELIVERANCE very unpleasant. Phil and Jill decide to move further south, perhaps to Ft. Lauderdale to check on the repairs to ROCINANTE.

In January, I receive a telephone call from Phil, saying he has been in touch with our Brazilian and has been hired by him to help with the repairs. He's calling to let me know the Brazilian knows absolutely nothing about what he's doing. Phil will try to keep him from completely botching the job. Fortunately a lot of the work, including the all important repainting of the hull, changing the color from white to black, is subcontracted to reputable boatyards. Every 2 or 3 weeks I get a telephone call from the Brazilian, asking for another check for $10,000. I'm too harassed in my construction business to do anything other that send him what he asks for.

ROCINANTE'S new paint job, Ft. Lauderdale, 1990

It's June, 1990, before the repairs to ROCINANTE are complete. All of the insurance money—plus more—has been spent, but some improvements have been added, including a new radar. Mary and I take our first vacation since Hugo and fly down to Ft Lauderdale. I must admit ROCINANTE looks beautiful in black, like a grand piano. Our last extravagance was the gold leaf lettering of her name on each side of her double ended stern. Mary and I, accompanied by two old friends but novice sailors, sail out of Bahia Mar at dusk, headed for West End, Bahamas. To us, the wind seems brisk and invigorating, but to our friends it's terrifying and life-threatening. The husband becomes sick, lurches below, breaking off the engine ignition key and passes out on a bunk. His wife sits frozen and wide eyed in the cockpit for the entire night. Everything is fine the next morning and we clear Customs in West End. Three days later we anchor in American Harbor, Man-O-War Cay, and move into Pirates Den.

Mary spends much of the summer at Pirates Den, entertaining a series of visitors. I return in late July to help sail ROCINANTE back to Charleston. Mary and I expect a pleasant sail home but, after the first day, a tropical storm forms in the western Atlantic, producing 25 to 30 knot winds from the north. We decide to tack across the Gulf Stream where we'll be closer to some port along the Florida coast. Waves in the Stream are 10 feet high and steep. We have too much head sail and no roller reefing genoa to shorten sail. We can roll up the genoa all the way, leaving the too small staysail as the only head sail. We need to take down the genoa and put up the smaller working jib. For an old guy, this is no easy task in 30 knots of wind and 10-foot seas.

Mary is at the helm. With the genoa furled she brings the bow into the wind and holds it there, using the engine. I allow the genoa to unfurl. As it flaps wildly I creep to the plunging bow, wearing a safety harness, loosen the genoa halyard and pull the thrashing sail down the track. Fortunately, it nests between the inside of the caprail and the trunk cabin and doesn't blow over the side. I wrap the sail with ties and fasten it to a rail. For the next 10 minutes I sort out parts of the bagged working jib, fastening the sheets, clipping the tack to the halyard by mistake, changing it, unwrapping and trying to align the luff tape to slide up the furling gear slot. Working with one hand and holding on with the other is making me very tired. It will take both of us to raise the jib. From the cockpit we back the staysail, haul in the main, and lock the wheel, so ROCINANTE will remain hove to. We both crawl to the base of the mast, wearing harnesses. I crawl out on the bow pulpit and guide the sail into the slot as Mary uses the halyard winch to hoist the flogging jib. We hurry back to the cockpit to sheet in the jib. The jib and staysail combination still gives us too much head sail for the wind we have, so I go forward again and take down the staysail. A reefed main and the working jib seem to be the right combination. I lie panting in the cockpit, totally exhausted. If we're going to make long ocean passages we need a good strong roller reefing genoa, so we can shorten sail without going back and forth to the bow. We'll get one once we're back in Charleston, along with the dodger and a replacement windvane and a few other things.

The wind has picked up to 35 knots and the swells are too much for the autopilot. We're taking a lot of water over the port rail. We take turns hand steering, bearing off as a big wave approaches, and surfing along as the wave lifts the keel and rolls under us. As night approaches, we're 35 miles off Jacksonville with gusts to 40 knots and 12-foot swells. We've never entered Mayport Inlet before but we have the charts. It's a straight forward approach with a marked jettied entrance. By midnight we're between the jetties, heading up the St. Johns River. Our destination is a marina close to where the river crosses the ICW. Suddenly, as we round a bend in the river we're looking straight into the bow of a huge floating structure, a barge full of automobiles being towed down the river by three tugs. The tugs are flashing their lights and blasting their horns and we barely get out of their way in time. We have to go under one drawbridge which is luckily still in operation at 0200. We go through the bridge and approach where the marina is supposed to be. There are no lights along the pier but, with the help of an outgoing tide and the right wind, we manage to slide into an empty slip, tie up and sleep for 8 hours. Next day the winds from Tropical Storm Bertha are still strong, so we work our way up the ICW for 4 days, to Charleston.

We've decided to take one additional shakedown cruise, both to prepare for our planned Atlantic crossing next spring and to escape the Carolinas for the rest of hurricane season. Mary and I leave Charleston in September, headed for the Chesapeake. We are sailing offshore to Beaufort, North Carolina, a 2-day passage. During the middle of the second night, off Frying Pan Shoals there's almost no wind. When I start the engine and shift into forward, there's a sound of loud thumping and grinding from the area of the transmission and no forward movement of the boat. Peering into the bilge with a flashlight, I'm startled to see the propeller shaft disconnected from the transmission and water pouring in around the shaft, where it passes through the stern. Worried that the shaft might shoot out through the stern and drop to the bottom, I hurriedly clamp some vice grips onto the shaft, pull the couplings back together and install some temporary bolts. Not wanting to take a chance on running the engine again, we change course for Southport, N.C. and sail with what little wind we have. The wind picks up and, by morning we're tied up at Southport Marina. A mechanic tells me the bolts weren't tight enough, which caused them to shear off. He replaces them with high strength bolts and we're back on our way.

Sailing north in Chesapeake Bay in October is no problem, other than being the butt of jokes from the many other boats sailing south. We continue north, stopping at Sarah's Creek, Fishing Bay, Urbanna, Irvington and Mobjack Bay, before crossing to the Eastern Shore. Anchored off Onancock, Virginia on November 1, we decide it's too cold without a diesel heater and that we should head for home.

A few mornings later, accompanied by twenty other southbound boats we leave the anchorage off Hospital Point at Norfolk, gawking at the Navy ships, and ridiculously racing to make the last pre-rush hour opening of a bridge. Ahead is a wall of fog across the ICW. We continue in zero visibility, following the boat ahead, afraid to slow down, lest we be run down from behind. The last thing I see before we run hard aground is a line of crab pots and the faint outline of some buildings on shore. Twenty minutes later the fog has lifted and we're distressed to learn ROCINANTE is half a mile out of the channel and very close to a chain link fence, enclosing several buildings marked U.S. Navy and Keep Out. Two men in a military police truck are shouting through a bullhorn that we must leave immediately. Unfortunately, we've run aground on a full moon high tide and the tide has already started falling. A few minutes later a Coast Guard cutter arrives to check our "watertight integrity" and give us the name of a towing company which they say we will surely need. We contact Capt. Lane Briggs of the towboat NORFOLK REBEL who says he'll try to pull us off on the evening high tide, if we haven't already worked our way off. Despite all attempts at kedging we need the NORFOLK REBEL and he backs in toward us, digging a channel with his prop. Capt. Lane and I admire each other's boats, his tug has sails in addition to the engine, and he tows us back to Hospital Point for a reasonable price. The next morning we set out again for home. By Nov. 15 we're back at Stono Marina in Charleston.

I'm working on two long lists of things to do to get ready for next spring's voyage. One list is related to work to be done to ROCINANTE such as the new jib, the diesel heater, the windvane self steering, completion of the dodger, repacking of the life raft, beefing up the battery charging system and a hundred other smaller items, all somewhat in process. The other list relates to disconnecting from "normal life," things like selling the house, transferring the construction business to my partner, finding someone to pay bills and many other necessary matters. I spent all of yesterday tracking down a lawyer I own a piece of property with, to tell him I'll be leaving and won't be able to continue our partnership. He was not happy. Today I'm in my office making flight arrangements for our family to make a last visit to Pirates Den at Man-O-War for the Christmas holidays, before we put it on the market. Mary will be working on ROCINANTE all day, getting ready to leave her, while we're at Man-O-War.

The telephone rings. It's Mary and she's almost in tears. Two sheriff's deputies knocked on the side of ROCINANTE a few minutes ago, handed her a ten page complaint signed by my lawyer partner and told her the boat will be sealed and remain in custody of the State until the complaint is satisfied. They are waiting for Mary to remove any personal gear before locking up ROCINANTE. I'm stunned, boiling, livid with rage. I tell Mary to wait there and not to worry. I promise to straighten it out and call her back. I call a lawyer I know, tell him it's an emergency and rush over to his office. He calls my lawyer partner and they discuss the complaint, which claims I reneged on a promise, have no other assets except a boat, and I intend to leave the country on the boat. I'm too angry to be allowed to talk. The lawyers negotiate a price to get me out of the partnership, the same price I offered to pay yesterday. I believe the bastard thinks it's a joke. I write a check, the complaint is satisfied and I call Mary and tell her it's OK.

It's May, 1991. Robert and Jamie will make the Atlantic crossing with us, satisfying ROCINANTE'S insurance carrier's requirement for a crew of four. Neither of them has a demanding job right now or any family responsibilities, and both badly want to go. Houses are sold and furniture is stored; Robert's girlfriend will handle paying our bills. Mary and I and ROCINANTE are as ready to go as we're ever going to be. After waiting one more day for the weather to be just right, we head almost due east from Charleston, toward Bermuda. The passage is too easy. Six days out of Charleston we're tied up at St. George's Dinghy Club, Bermuda.

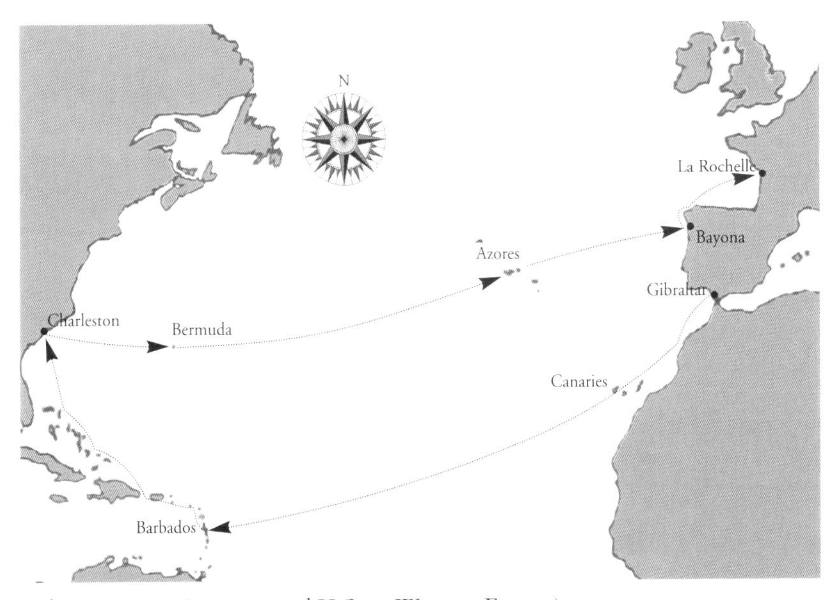

Atlantic Ocean (east coast of U.S. to Western Europe)

A few months ago I paid a fee to join the annual Trans Arc Rally from Bermuda to the Azores, organized by British sailor Jimmy Cornell, thinking we would feel more secure in company with a hundred boats, rather than being alone. We're to have free marina slips at both ends of the journey, some social activities and daily checks on each boat's position and condition. Robert and Jamie think we've made a mistake and should just strike out, alone. Robert and I have an ongoing disagreement about philosophies of sailing. I maintain that the pleasure of a successful passage is derived from going from place "A" to place "B" as efficiently and safely as possible. Robert thinks that, having departed from "A," the maximum pleasure comes from encountering excitement and danger, regardless of arrival at "B." We wait and attend a weather summary, which advises we will probably need to sail north of the rhumb line to Horta to find sufficient wind. On May 25 we cross the starting line with just twenty other sailboats, to the accompaniment of a bagpiper on the Committee boat. After the first day, with the predicted absence of wind, boats are scattering to find more favorable conditions. At reporting time on the second morning our VHF radio is barely in range to report our position to the "mother boat." We listen to other boats reporting on their long range single sideband radios but we have only an inexpensive SSB receiver and no transmitter.

We decide to venture further north to find more wind. It's our third day out of Bermuda. A sea fog has set in and there are isolated gusts of wind. Robert, our most experienced crew, has a premonition of bad weather ahead—mostly based on having bananas on board and not being able to catch any fish. During the night, the wind picks up to 30 knots out of the northwest. We're running downwind with a reefed main and no head sail. The barometer has fallen 20 milibars and the NOAA high seas forecast tells of an intensifying low pressure system with winds of 35 to 40 knots and 15-foot seas.

The waves have built to the height of a two-story house. Waves pile on top of waves, curling over and becoming translucent green. Some rear up alongside, roar like a lion and speed off into the distance. They lift us up and surf us down their curling faces. Some waves jump the sternrail and crash down onto the dodger or into the cockpit. We're steering by hand in 2 hour watches, wearing our heaviest oilskins and safety harnesses. I'm on watch, trying to avoid the meanest looking waves, when a big one thunders into our port side, washing away Robert's favorite fishing lures and half filling the cockpit basin with sea water.

I am 57 today. My birthday present is a dinner of beanie weanies, soda crackers and a beer, plus relief from standing a night watch. For 3 days and nights we've been battling this gale, still making pretty good time towards Horta. The new roller reefing jib is working well, holding its shape no matter how much we have to roll it up. Robert and Jamie are using every combination of sails. When the sail track fasteners begin to pop off the double reefed main, they take it down and put up the storm trysail for the first time. Last spring Jamie and I had mounted a separate track on the mast for

Drying out the gear, view from the spreaders, near Horta, 1991

the trysail, drilling and tapping almost a hundred screws, hoping we'd never have to use it.

We still listen to the SSB frequency that the Trans Arc boats use to talk to each other. Last night one of them broadcast a "pan-pan," saying his rudder shaft had sheared off and he had no steering. Another boat was on the way to help him. Then there was another "pan-pan" from a Dutch boat, whose captain had had a mental "collapse." The rest of his crew wanted him off their boat. A British boat with a doctor on board was to rendezvous and transfer the berserk captain.

Today the wind is beginning to subside. We're less than 600 miles from Horta and should be there in 4 or 5 days. The sun is out for the first time and everyone is trying to dry out their gear. We've seen no other boats since the first day but this morning I'm having a VHF radio conversation with a Brit on a 30-foot catamaran. He and his wife and baby are returning to England. We agree it was quite a gale—Force 9, he says. I'm getting a call from someone on another boat, who has overheard our conversation. He's in sight of us and wants a fix on his position. He took a knockdown a few nights ago and lost his electronics. He's a Polish sailboat, SOLIDARITY, on his way from Chicago to Poland, via the Azores.

We are 15 days out of Bermuda and we can see the island of Faial ahead. We have no idea of how many Trans Arc boats have already finished but one of them, KVACK, is merging with us. The wind is dying. I think we both fear we may be the last boat to finish. We both start our engines and leisurely motor sail. We're creeping toward the finish line. Now, we're both speeding up, obviously racing to be first. Smoke is pouring from our exhausts. ROCINANTE rounds in, close to an ancient volcano crater, cuts inside and finishes a boat length ahead. We tie up outside of Horta harbor, embarrassed to find out only eleven Trans Arc boats are already here. We've sailed about 2000 miles, counting our wanderings before the gale, in just under 15 days.

Chapter 7

Rocinante in England and Ireland

The Azores Islands are most beautiful, and made more interesting by the fact you have to sail so far to enjoy them. After all of the Trans Arc participants have finished, we attend a drunken victory party at Peter's Sport Bar, the international center of activity for all sailing visitors to Horta. The last boat to finish had lost all wind, its engine failed to start, it accepted a tow from a Portuguese fishing vessel and the owner now faces the possibility of having to pay an $8000 towing fee.

Trans Arc party, Peters Sports Bar, Horta, Azores

The next day Mary paints a copy of the bizarre ROCINANTE horse, which Charlie had painted on our windvane, on a concrete pillar at the marina, a tradition for all boats visiting Horta. We've become friends with the crews of many boats from all over Europe and America, who weathered the storm. We help each other repair broken gear and get ready for the next leg of our respective journeys. After a week in Horta, we sail 70 miles to anchor in the harbor off the town of Angra Du Heroismo on the island of Terceira, where a food and music festival is in progress. We spend a week here, eating and drinking well, enjoying the music and attending a bullfight. On June 27 we leave Terceira, headed for the mainland of Spain.

Mary paints ROCINANTE'S totem

We're tied up at the yacht club marina at Bayona, Spain, after a slow, hot and uneventful 800 mile, 8-day passage. Bayona is a swinging place with lots of young people and much to do. I can sense Robert and Jamie's frustrations at being in such a place and not having their own boat, plenty of money and a knowledge of the Spanish language. I believe they're getting homesick, and we've still got a long way to go before they fly back from England. I'll keep them from starving but I may not be able to keep them in beer. We stay in Bayona for a week, buying charts for the northwest coast of Spain and taking a bus trip to Santiago de Compostella, the most important city in the region.

Leaving Terceira, Azores, headed for Spain

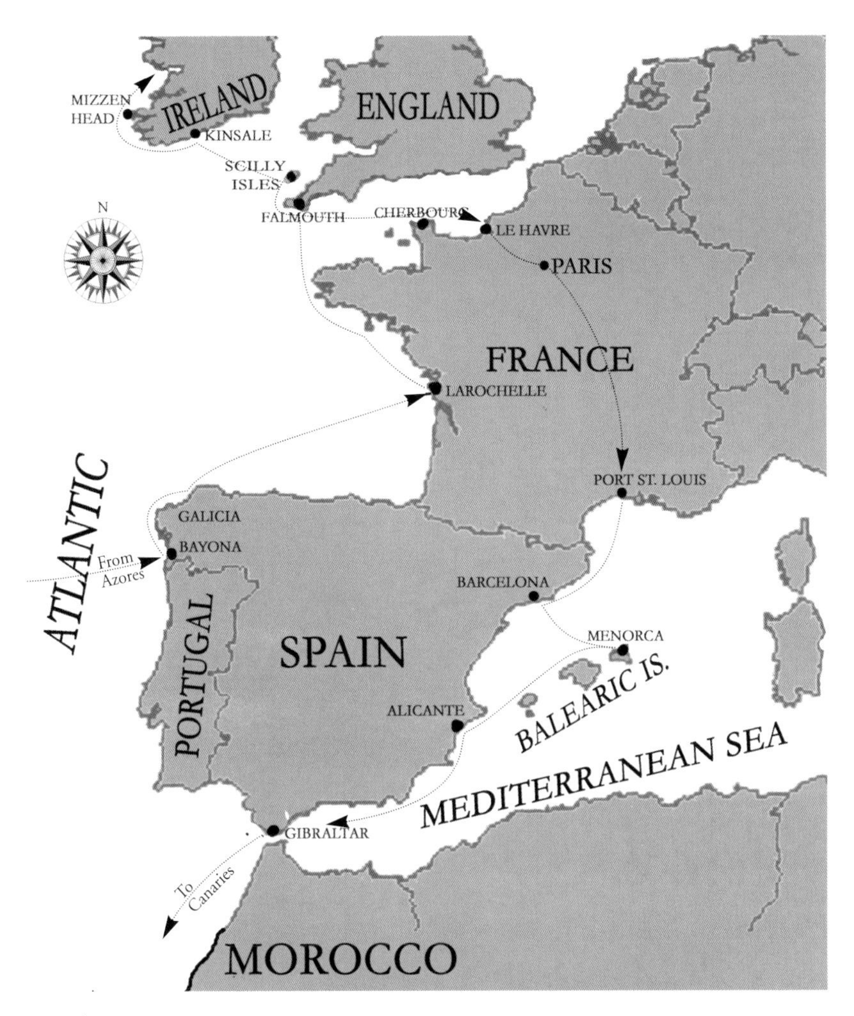

Northwestern Europe

We're day sailing north, along the coast of Galicia, from one Ria to the next. The Rias are like fjords, bays between the rugged mountains of the mainland. Each Ria has its own little fishing village, with winding streets and ancient stone churches, Calvaries, and horreroes, distinctive stone grain storage warehouses on stilts.We anchor and explore each village—Combarro, Caraminal and Muros. There aren't many tourists here. At Caraminal the captain of an Irish sailboat that is anchored near ROCINANTE invites us over for "a little drink." The whole family is aboard—husband, wife, three daughters and a son—all near enough our own family's ages. They've cruised in Galicia before, so we accompany them to a restaurant in Muros where both our families celebrate Mary and Deirdre's birthdays, eating paella and drinking cheap Rioja wine, which turns our teeth blue. We part company with them at Muros but promise to sail to Cork next year to see them. We continue north to Corcubian and, from there, round Cape Finisterre, the westernmost point of continental Europe. It's much windier here and we're glad to tuck into an anchorage off the town of Camarinas.

We've been pinned down here for 2 days by heavy northeast winds, waiting for a break to sail on to La Coruna. I'm sitting at a small outdoor cafe bar crowded with local fishermen, watching the Sunday afternoon strollers promenade. I'm noticed as a stranger and the man next to me, who speaks both English and Spanish, listens as I explain we're a family who have sailed from America on our boat and are here on vacation. He tells the others in Spanish what I have said. The fishermen look at me like I'm crazy and loudly talk back and forth to each other. After a minute my neighbor translates what's being said. "They say they would never cross an ocean in a boat for pleasure, only for money. That one says the ocean is a dangerous place, whose surface is too soft to walk on and whose air is too thick to breathe. He says the town has lost more than twenty fishermen drowned this year. He says for you to look around at the many women in mourning. Even so, he says, because we are so poor there are plenty of men ready to take the places of those who drowned." I get their point and wish I could do more than just sympathize that so many have died. They seem to like me more when I tell them the name of our boat is ROCINANTE, a name they all recognize.

The next morning the weather is somewhat improved, but I'm for waiting another day. It's raining and I'm a little timid about cruising along what the Spanish charts note as "The Coast of Death." The boys want to go on, and the issue is settled when a British boat sails by, shouting "See you in La Coruna." Just before dark we take a mooring off the yacht club in this large industrial city at the northwest corner of Spain. Here, we prepare to set off across the Bay of Biscay toward La Rochelle, France, 375 miles away.

It's the second night of our passage to La Rochelle. The Bay of Biscay has acquired a somewhat nasty reputation, mostly based on problems square riggers had trying to beat against prevailing winds that would push them across the bay and onto the rocks of the French coast. There's not much wind tonight but we don't want to run the engine unless we have to. We've continued to have problems with the alternator belt, sheave and bracket ever since the electrician in Charleston installed an alternator larger than the one that came with the engine. Yesterday the steel bracket broke in half, and we jury rigged something with a wooden wedge to keep tension on the belt.

The wind has dropped to almost nothing so I reluctantly tell Mary to go ahead and crank the engine. When she does, sparks start to fly from the engine compartment and smoke begins to pour out along with with the smell of burning insulation. All of our electrical systems are shorted out and we're in total darkness, except for the sparks. We open up the engine compartment and look in with a flashlight. Sparks continue to fly and smoke billows, threatening to become a full fledged fire. I yell for Robert to grab a fire extinguisher and squirt it onto the engine. When he does, the smoke becomes much thicker and more acrid but there are no flames. I can see a wooden wedge has been driven on top of an electrical wire and caused the short. I take a hammer and knock out the wedge, which stops the sparks. Slowly, smoke clears. We have power again for the navigation and cabin lights. The engine is covered with white powder from the fire extinguisher. I realize now we should have used the halon extinguisher instead of a dry chemical one, but it's too late now. It will require a massive cleanup, later. We'll just have to wait for some wind and sail the rest of the way. We've still got 225 miles to go. Mary admits this was the first time she ever thought, "Life raft!"

The wind has picked up dramatically and we're making over seven knots on a beam reach. The backstay hums as it always does when the wind blows 25 knots. We want to approach La Rochelle in daylight but our speed puts us in sight of land 3 hours before daylight. We don't have very good charts of this harbor or up to date tide tables, and we know from the cruising guide that there is less than 6 feet over the bar at low tide. We heave to and wait for daylight. Just before sunrise we watch a gray patrol boat approach us and stop. A big black Zodiac dinghy is put over the side and three uniformed French Customs agents zoom alongside us and request to come aboard. They're very polite but spend a half hour searching ROCINANTE from stem to stern. All that time we're drifting back with the tide, away from our destination. They're finally satisfied, apologizing for our inconvenience and signing our log so we won't be searched again in French waters. They give us the time of high tide and we beat our way back toward the entrance. We've already experimented with cranking the engine and it seems to be OK. The shorted out wire led to the magnetic engine cutoff, so shutting down the engine may be a problem when we get there. We motor up the channel toward the twin medieval towers that guard the city center. The huge marina is a mile before the city center. We're directed by the dockmaster into one of the three thousand slips.

The first priority is to find a new magnetic cutoff switch for the engine and find someone to make a new alternator bracket. The city is full of yachting activity, chandleries and repair facilities, but it's August and it seems all of France is on vacation. I find a machine shop that's open but all of the workmen are on vacation except one welder, who says he can't make a new bracket but can try to reweld the old one. He doesn't have a magnetic switch and doesn't know where to find one. Another customer in the shop, a young man about my age, takes an interest in the burned up cutoff and tells me, if I will go home with him, he will make a replacement. We drive to his house and, within a few minutes, he's turned the old magnetic cutoff into a manual one, which will allow us to shut down the engine by pulling a wire. He drives to the marina and helps install the cutoff. He won't take any money and I don't know how to thank him, but he seems pleased to be of help.

La Rochelle is a bustling tourist city, a continuous summer festival. We experience wonderful French food, wine and style for the first time. We tour many sights and explore the countryside on bikes, waiting for the bracket to be welded. Robert and Jamie particularly enjoy exploring the ruins of the World War II German submarine pens and the German command center in the basement of a hotel, left as if the officers had abandoned it only yesterday.

The rewelded bracket holds for a day, as we sail to Les Sables d'Olonne but, the next day, on our way along the Atlantic coast toward the island of Île d'Yeu, it breaks again and we have to resort to the wooden wedge. The tide range at Île d'Yeu is almost 20 feet. Without a lock, the port town of Joinville would be too shallow to be usable at low tide. The lock, which is opened only at high tide to let boats in and out, traps water in a basin. We enter the basin through the lock on the afternoon high tide and find it full of fishing and pleasure boats. We don't know what to do about tying up but are told by the captain of a British sailboat to raft up outside of him and two other boats, tied to the wall. For the first time we experience the accepted practice of rafting up and crossing other boats to get to shore.

We're here to visit a French couple we met years ago while sailing in the Bahamas, who own a house here and one in Paris. They quickly find a man to make a sturdy new bracket, which solves our problem. We explore small and picturesque Île d'Yeu, which is crowded with tourists who are ferried over from the mainland each day. Twice every 24 hours, at high tide, cruising boats and fishing boats enter and leave Joinville through the lock, shifting positions in the rafts of boats, like playing musical chairs in the crowded basin. A man in a small wooden boat beside us, a British "Old Gaffer," tells me he's seen Phil and Jill on their boat, DELIVERANCE, who are waiting for us to rendezvous a little further north.

Today, we're headed for the larger island of Belle Île, 60 miles from Île d'Yeu, where we hope to find DELIVERANCE. We arrive at 0300, tying on to a giant mooring ball just off the entrance to the harbor. We wait until a reasonable hour and then call DELIVERANCE over and over on the VHF but get no answer. This part of Brittany is full of cruising boats and it'll be very difficult to find any one boat. We decide to proceed further north. In the afternoon, just as we're passing Île de Groix, DELIVERANCE calls on the radio, saying ROCINANTE is in sight of where they're anchored. We follow them to a marina in the town of Lorient, where there's a grand reunion, including Phil and Jill's son and his fiancé, friends of Robert and Jamie.

We plan to cruise the rest of the way to Falmouth in Cornwall in company with DELIVERANCE. A friend of Phil's, Laurie, will also cruise along on his boat, JAHOE. We continue next day along the rugged rocky coast of Brittany, the Côte Sauvage, to Loctudy to visit with other French friends. From here, via the turbulent Raz passage, we sail into a cove and anchor near the town of Camaret. Concrete ruins of German World War II gun emplacements look down from cliffs surrounding the cove.

Tonight the crews of ROCINANTE, DELIVERANCE and JAHOE are eating lamb shish kebab and drinking quantities of cheap French wine around a driftwood bonfire on a stony beach. In the cove where our dinghies are tied, the surf from a rising tide moves sizable round stones back and forth with a loud grinding noise. Behind our narrow beach, a cliff rises straight up 100 feet. We must launch our dinghies into the rock-rolling surf before the rising tide eliminates our beach. We joke about having to climb the cliff to escape. Wet, full of food and slightly drunk, we manage a return to our respective boats, and sleep well.

It's a hundred mile passage from L'Aberlidut, on the French side of the Channel, to Falmouth. We get underway at dawn in dense fog with almost no wind. ROCINANTE is the only boat with radar. On our radar screen we watch a steady stream of freighters proceeding up and down the English Channel in their lanes of traffic, occasionally warning our friends of a close one. Approaching the Cornish coast late the next night, we aren't able to see the powerful Lizard light at all. We almost run into the red occulting light at St. Anthony Head, Falmouth, before we see it. DELIVERANCE guides us through the rocky entrance to an anchorage off St. Mawes. The next day we clear English Customs and check into a new, locked in marina at Point Pendennis, Falmouth, where we will spend the winter. After four months and 4500 miles Robert and Jamie leave ROCINANTE, take a bus to London and catch a Virgin Airlines flight home. They've learned a lot, including obeying Mary's command to keep the toilet seat down.

Fall and winter here are cold, damp, windy and depressing, even though the Brits call Cornwall the Riviera of England. ROCINANTE is a cozy haven from the weather, with her diesel and electric heaters going, except for the continuing problem of condensation on the inside of the hull. I can see why the Brits spend a lot of time in pubs, drinking bitters and trying to keep warm in front of coal fires. On this typical Sunday afternoon we're sipping our Beamish pints and looking out the window of our favorite pub, The Ship, at the rough gray Channel and jagged rocks, whipped by rain and wind from another cold front passing across England. During every brief period of brightness, we take the opportunity to visit the many attractions of rugged Cornwall, driving the old Russian Lada sedan we bought here along the very narrow hedge-lined rural roads. For additional diversion and self-punishment, I work 1 or 2 days a week in a stone quarry, chipping granite beach boulders into crude head shapes for a local monumental mason. We've made many friends here, including a hardy group who play tennis twice a week, throughout the winter, in spite of the weather.

We're overjoyed when spring finally arrives. Mary's father and his lady friend visit us in April and we tour much of Scotland and northern England in our Lada. Each evening of the trip I wrestle four big suitcases up two or three flights of stairs to some 17th century B&B bedroom and, each morning I try to wedge the same suitcases into our tiny trunk. We've put over 12,000 miles on the old beige rattletrap since last fall, visiting Southampton for the boat show, London twice (Greenwich, clipper ship CUTTY SARK, Chichester's GIPSY MOTH, St. Katherines Docks), Bristol (Brunel's SS GREAT BRITAIN, National Lifeboat Museum), Portsmouth (Nelson's VICTORY, Henry VIII's MARY ROSE) and every other monument from Stonehenge to Westminster Abbey.

ROCINANTE and FLEXEN anchored off St. Agnes, Scilly Isles

In mid-May, we move ROCINANTE to an anchorage in the Helferd River and then join DELIVERANCE for a cruise to the Scilly Isles, five inhabited rocky islands 60 miles off the coast of Cornwall. The Scillies are a graveyard for many ships, including the entire flotilla of England's infamous Admiral Cloudsley Shovel, who tried to round the southwest tip of England in fog. We sail downwind, wing and wing past Wolf Rock and on toward the largest island, St. Mary's. Phil and Jill, accompanied on DELIVERANCE by another English couple, meet us at St Mary's Pool, the only real harbor in the islands. For a week they show us the hidden tiny harbors and anchorages of these little magic flower-covered islands. Our favorite is St. Agnes, where we race up a hill to the Turks Head pub each noon, trying to get ahead of the day trippers from St. Mary's, to have a pint of Murphy's and order pasties, meat and potato pies that the Cornish tin miners took down into the mines for lunch. Mary and I stay in The Scillies another 2 weeks before leaving Tresco Channel for Ireland.

It's a 140 mile overnight sail from The Scillies to Kinsale, Ireland. The spectacularly beautiful green hills of Southwest Ireland are in view by early afternoon. We sail round the Old Head of Kinsale and up the River Bandon to anchor in front of Kinsale Yacht Club. Our Irish friends, whom we had met in Spain last summer, have reserved a slip for us here. We visit with them in Cork and take a side trip to Dublin by train, before leaving to explore the southwest coast.

We travel west, making day trips to protected anchorages off the rivers and bays—Glandore, Union Hall and Castletownsend, where we rendezvous with our friends on MOSHULU II. We accompany them to the tiny shallow harbor at Clear Island and walk up the hill to have a "loose pint" at Paddy O'Shea's, the southwesternmost pub in all of Ireland. From there we visit Schull, Baltimore and Crookhaven, before rounding Mizzen Head and turning north. Because there's not much wind in the protected harbor at Crookhaven, we tow our inflatable dinghy behind ROCINANTE instead of lifting it on deck. When we clear the protection of the hills, we're facing a 20 knot headwind and some sizable Atlantic swells. We tack back and forth to clear the rips off the towering rocky cliffs of Mizzen Head, bashing about in a most uncomfortable way. It's a big relief when we finally clear the headland and ease off to a comfortable reach across Bantry

Bay, toward Bear Island. We can see the forward section of the dinghy slowly deflating, punctured by too much pressure from the towline. We pass through a narrow entrance and anchor off the commercial fishing port of Castletown Bere.

Castletown Bere is different from the other towns we've visited. There's no marina or facility for pleasure boats and no tourists. This is a working fishing town with commercial chandleries and a boatyard for hauling big boats. There are many pubs here but the center of social activity for cruising sailors seems to be Mary McCarthy's Grocery and Pub. Caroline and Mandy meet us at Mary McCarthy's to deliver some mail from the USA. They introduce us to Adrienne, the attractive owner, who had abandoned a nursing career in Dublin to take over the grocery and pub when her uncle died. At the front of the building she fills orders for box loads of groceries being delivered to fishing boats, provisioning for trips. At the back she draws pints of Murphys and Guinness for fishermen and sailors. On one afternoon, as we sit in the back of Mary McCarthy's, an unscheduled concert takes place, with performers on fiddle, accordion, guitar and tambourine drum playing traditional Irish music.

View of the hills of Adrigole, Ireland

After almost a week of rain we leave Castletown Bere and sail up Bantry Bay to Glengariff, and then to a beautiful isolated little bay at Adrigole, where we can see a waterfall tumbling down Thomas Hardy's Hungry Hill. We motor the dinghy across a bay, past three seals sunning on a low tide rock. We take a long walk up a mountain road and back across the wild countryside of abandoned stone churches, Ogham stones and fields of cows and sheep. We spend the next night anchored in front of one of the famous Glennan sailing schools, at Lawrence Cove; then sail, at slack tide, through the narrow cut between Dursey Island and the mainland, to the mouth of the Kenmare River.

We're making the approach to an anchorage at Derrynane, motor sailing up a narrow rocky channel off the Kenmare River, marked by a range formed by two masonry towers. We have an Irish Coast Pilot which tells us to align the towers to avoid sunken ledges of rock on both sides of the channel. I interpret the chart as saying we must pass the second tower's port side before turning to starboard, into the deeper cove. Mary disagrees and, just as we pass the second tower she insists we're supposed to turn before the second tower. By this time the depth gauge has gone down from ten to eight to six feet and I see nothing but rocks under us. I make a wild turn to starboard, waiting for a crunch and, seconds later we slip into deep water. She was right and we've been lucky again. From now on we'll check each other's chart interpretation and agree before we make an approach like that.

At the Derrynane anchorage, we contract with a fishing boat to take us out to inaccessible Great Skellig Island, one of two steep jagged cones of offshore rock, rising 700 feet above the sea. Our captain approaches the landing ledge and we jump off the heaving boat. He allows us 2 hours to climb the 600 stone steps carved into the mountain 1500 years ago, and to visit the abandoned monastery. The few monks who lived here were self sufficient in spite of the difficult conditions. Huts and a church were built of stones with no mortar, a walled plot of thin soil grew food, a flat rock collected water and trenches in the rock buried the dead. Unfortunately, we're part of a steady stream of summer visitors with snapping and grinding cameras, wearing down the steps and disturbing nesting puffins and other rare birds. As we return to ROCINANTE, we pass near the smaller

Skellig Island, stained almost white by guano from thousands of gannets who live there.

We sail further up the Kenmare River to Sneem and then across to an anchorage in front of the town of Kilmakilloge. The wind is strong and we put down two anchors before we feel safe leaving ROCINANTE. A fellow American greets us in the pub at the base of the pier, saying he saw our U.S. ensign, the first one in years, from the porch of his house. After a serious operation, he and his wife had retired to this isolated but beautiful spot.

The furthest north we sail is Dingle, where we're greeted by the town's resident dolphin, Fungie. We stay for a few days in this pleasant tourist town that boasts 52 pubs—but by mid-August we feel it is time to start back before we miss the end of sailing season. We make longer offshore passages back toward Kinsale, taking time to photograph each other with Fastnet Lighthouse close in the background. We tie up at Kinsale Yacht Club on August 23, 1992.

Sailing past Fastnet Light

The weather has taken a turn for the worse. We need to get back to Falmouth to meet son Charlie, who is due on September 4. From Falmouth, we plan to cross the English Channel to Le Havre and motor up the Seine to Paris for the winter. We run into a sailing couple we met in

Cornwall last winter, who also are waiting for good weather to return to Falmouth. Ron has a Weatherfax on his boat and we review the printed forecasts every morning. On Sunday he says, "I think Tuesday is the day. The wind's supposed to die down from 30 to 20 and back to 30 or more on Thursday. By that time we'll have caught the right tide around The Lizard and will already be in Falmouth. It's our window of opportunity. This one chart, here, called 'Sea State' must be a mistake. It shows 3 to 5 meter swells in the Celtic Sea. That must be a misprint." I'm doubtful, but I nod slightly and say, "Umm".

The Monday BBC shipping forecast is for Force 5 to 7 in our area. The Tuesday morning forecast is ambiguous, possible Force 8 gale approaching, possibly tomorrow. It's a toss-up but, when Ron's boat and another one throw off their docking lines, we do the same. We have 25 to 30 knots on the beam, with 10-foot seas, from the beginning. We're roaring along at over 6 knots with a reefed main and a little bit of jib. We talk back and forth on the VHF with Ron's wife, who says he is pretty seasick and in his bunk. Night comes on early and the wind drops below 25 knots. I put up the staysail and take in a little on the jib. After a squall passes through, with gusts over 40, the clouds part and the sky is full of stars and a sliver of the moon. The wind becomes steady enough to use windvane steering. The midnight shipping forecast definitely calls for gales in the English Channel all day Wednesday, closing our window of opportunity for getting around The Lizard. Before the gray dawn I see reflections on the cloud bottoms from the light at Seven Stones Lightship, and faint flashes from Bishop's Rock Light, both protecting the Scillies. I talk with Ron about alternate UK harbors between Lands End and The Lizard, and we decide to go for Newlyn, a fishing port in Mount's Bay.

On Wednesday morning, winds increase to a steady 35 knots, with gusts to 50. After the winds come torrents of rain, flattening the waves. We beat our way toward Wolf Rock, marking the northwest entrance to the English Channel. Container ships are wallowing in heavy seas. I grip the helmsman's seat with my knees and fight the wheel to hold our course, as wind drives waves across the cockpit and rain pours down my collar. What will happen if I get too tired to keep on doing this or what if I have a cramp or pull a muscle or what if my hat shrinks so much I faint? What if the wind keeps increasing and I have to go forward to shorten sail or what if a shroud gives way or the main rips? Actually, we're doing pretty well. When we turn toward the entrance to Mount's Bay with its conical peak in the distance, the wind is behind us and we roll down the swells at 6 knots. We turn into Newlyn Harbor and join the many other yachts and fishing boats sheltering from the gale. We tie up on the outside of a raft of ten other boats.

Rafted up in Newlyn, Cornwall

Two days later the wind drops and we sail around The Lizard and into Falmouth harbor. Fall is in the air and sailing season is almost over. I could have been happy this winter, sitting in front of a peat fire with a Penguin paperback, a BBC concert and a bottle of Paddys, looking out some rain-spattered window across the green hills of Ireland.

Chapter 8

Rocinante in France and Spain

When Charlie arrives in Falmouth on September 5, we say our goodbyes to friends and, on Sunday, sail up the Channel to Newton Ferrers, a tiny pleasure harbor tucked into the hills near Plymouth, where the locals are taking their last sails of the season. Next day, we're on our way toward Le Havre, 180 miles east.

Channel sailing is a new and tricky business for us, with much progress depending on the strong easterly and westerly currents shown in daily Current Tables, which we have. We do pretty well the first day, crossing toward the coast of France, even though Charlie pays the price by being seasick again. As night comes on, the wind dies. We must continue to make progress against the currents in order to get to Le Havre by tomorrow night, so I crank the engine. Five minutes later the oil pressure alarm begins to ring and I shut down the engine, check the oil level and see there is no oil. I make a guess that the oil cooler must have ruptured and all of the oil was pumped overboard. We're making slow progress under sail and beginning to be swept toward the Channel Islands by the Alderney Current. This will never do. We check for an alternate port and decide on Cherbourg, only 30 miles away. By changing course we have a more favorable wind and are making 5 knots toward Cherbourg. About 2400, we can see a powerful occulting green light marking the entrance to Cherbourg's outer harbor. We don't have a very detailed chart of the harbor and are surprised how huge it is, 2 miles across. We sail across the outer harbor toward what is supposed to be a pleasure boat basin. We sail through that entrance and tie up to a floating pier at 0200.

The Cherbourg Marina is a big one with all services, including a mechanic, who confirms my suspicion about the engine oil cooler and orders a new one from Germany. During the 2 weeks it will take to receive and install the new oil cooler, we have time to work on a few other boat problems. Charlie and I are attacking the most unpleasant one today. During the past year, the size of the opening in the sanitary discharge hose from the head has become smaller and smaller, due to a buildup of calcium on the inside surface of the hoses—and now it's plugged up entirely. The only remedy at this point is to try and disconnect and remove the hoses and clean them out. Metric sized hoses, available here, won't fit. We spend the entire morning on our stomachs reaching way back under the cabin sole with screwdrivers, loosening hose clamps and pulling and twisting the hoses until finally, there's an explosive release of pressure and a big mess to be cleaned up later. We finally have all of the disconnected hoses out on the pier. After washing them off we beat them on the dock and pound them with hammers, until messy chunks fall off the hose walls and out the ends. By the time we get it all back together and clean up, we've killed a whole day.

After such a stressful day, Charlie and I decide to explore the night life of Cherbourg, the first French city liberated by the Americans during World War II. We are surprised to discover the Alabama Bar and Cafe, which is decorated with U.S. Civil War artifacts and Rebel flags. The bartender tells us the Confederate ship, CSS ALABAMA, after sinking 65 union ships was sunk by the USS KEARSARGE off Cherbourg in 1864. We might have learned more if it hadn't been for a drunken Frenchman in the bar, who continued to scream obscenities at us as the bartender apologized and told us to pay no attention to him. During the next 2 weeks, we rent a car and explore the D-Day Normandy beaches and Mont St. Michel, and drive to see the Bayeux tapestry depicting the Norman invasion of 1066. We drive over to Rouen to check out the facility for removing ROCINANTE'S mast.

Charlie not feeling well, mouth of Seine

The replacement oil cooler finally arrives and the mechanic and I install it. On October 1, we sail past the D-Day beaches to Le Havre. We're now in a real hurry because our reservation at the Arsenal Marina in Paris was for arrival on October 1. The 60-mile trip up the tidal River Seine from Le Havre to Rouen has to be started just before the beginning of an incoming tide. It would be impossible for us to motor against the tidal current. We get underway from Le Havre Marina at 0600 in 30 knots of northeast wind and rain, motoring across 8-foot swells in the Seine estuary, rolling 30 degrees, side to side, and making Charlie seasick for the last time. We finally round a bend into calmer water, and are making good time with the current. We don't quite make it to Rouen before the tide changes and darkness catches us. Charlie spots a mooring buoy near a ferry slip and we latch onto it for the night. The next day we motor into Darse de Docks, where a tower crane removes ROCINANTE'S mast. We leave the mast here for the winter and tie up at Rouen Marina, already closed for the season. It takes three more days to motor up the Seine, passing through six big mechanized locks. The wide winding river is very beautiful and has little current between Rouen and Paris.

ROCINANTE approaching the Eiffel Tower, 1992

Approaching the center of Paris by boat for the first time is a thrilling experience for us, maneuvering through commercial river traffic and Bateau Mouches full of passengers, passing under ornate bridges lined with waving tourists and hurrying pedestrians, and motoring past the Eiffel Tower and Notre Dame Cathedral. We tie up to a little floating pier on the right bank of the Seine and telephone the Arsenal Marina dockmaster. The lock is opened and we're lifted 10 feet up into the marina basin. Although it's already October 12, our reservation is honored and we're assigned a space for the winter. Arsenal Marina is a two block long basin located in the center of Paris, between the right bank of the Seine and the Place de la Bastille Metro station. The basin extends under the Place de la Bastille and emerges beyond it as part of Canal St. Martin. Its quays and floating piers are 40 feet below the traffic noise of busy streets that are lined with shops and five story apartment buildings. Two hundred yachts and barges fill the basin, which was built in the 14th century as part of a moat surrounding Charles V's fortified residence, the Bastille.

ROCINANTE is tied up outside a pretty Dutch barge, VERTROUWEN, owned by a couple from Texas. They help us solve the problems of connecting French electricity and propane to ROCINANTE'S American fittings. We learn the peculiarities of mail delivery, telephoning, paying bills and using the unisex showers tucked into a niche in a stone wall, where Metro trains rumble a few feet overhead. We meet the crews of the other three American sailboats wintering at the Arsenal. Mary's French is good enough to get us through initial difficulties of finding bank machines, grocery and department stores, laundromats, boulangeries, open air markets and kiosks selling Herald Tribunes and Pariscopes. Also, our French sailing friends and two Parisian girl architect friends are helpful and able to give Charlie some space in their atelier to work on his paintings. Charlie becomes almost independent, living his own life in Paris as a starving artist and using ROCINANTE as a base.

Charlie needs some lumber to make canvas stretchers for the big paintings he usually creates. He finds a lumber yard on our side of the Seine a few blocks down river. We walk along the quay, without having to cross any streets, to the busy yard where blue clad workmen load lumber into heavy construction trucks with forklifts. No one seems to notice us and I find a big stack of long metric 2 x 4's and a sheet of plywood to make gussets for the stretcher corners. I stack what we want in a pile but nobody pays any attention to us. Finally Charlie and I carry our load to the door of an office in a construction trailer and I go inside seeking—to no avail—someone who speaks a little English. Five clerks are filling out forms, talking on telephones and to each other. Making persistent use of sign language and my very limited French, I convince one French clerk to look at our little pile, make out an invoice and accept my francs. Charlie and I load the pile onto our shoulders and slowly make our way along the river, under a railroad trestle, across the lock gate and back to The Arsenal. On ROCINANTE'S pier we saw out the four by eight foot frames and screw the corners together. They're too large to fit into the Metro, so Charlie lugs them, one at a time, a mile and a half to the atelier, where he stretches and staples his canvas and begins to paint.

We're finding it easy to travel most anywhere in Paris by Metro. The Bastille station, a labyrinth of tubes running out in all directions, is less than a hundred yards from ROCINANTE. Most mornings, in good weather or bad, mostly bad, we grab our dog-eared Paris Michelin Guide, umbrellas, backpacks and Mary's cameras and board the Metro, bound for another museum, church, park or market. We think we'll visit everything listed in the Michelin Guide before spring. Charlie and I visit a few bizarre places together, with and without Mary, including a concert in a dark room at the Pompidou Center in which three men, unaccompanied by instruments, pop their jaws and whistle experimentally; the annual international insect exhibit in tents in the park at Vincennes; a guided tour of the Paris sewers; a three hour bagpipe concert; an indoor American football game between the Orlando Semi-pros and the European Allstars; and a loud percussion concert at the new Opera House. During the winter, Mary and I take side trips to Chartres and Brittany. We entertain several friends from Great Britain, Ireland and the United States. We fly home once for 3 weeks for me to give my goddaughter away at the most elaborate wedding in the postbellum history of South Carolina, returning to Paris with a new global positioning system (GPS) and new hoses for ROCINANTE'S head. Charlie returns to South Carolina in late February, declaring he's had a great time. For us it's an exciting winter in the City of Light.

We've changed our minds about this spring's itinerary. Originally, we'd planned to return to the mouth of the Seine, visit the Channel Islands and sail around Portugal and Spain to Gibraltar. Now we've learned that we can carry ROCINANTE'S 6-foot draft through the French canals, down the Rhone River to the Mediterranean Sea, and south along the Spanish coast to Gibraltar. We've been told the canals are well worth a visit. We leave Arsenal Marina on April 1, 1993, and travel down the Seine to retrieve the mast and place it on deck. We return once more through Paris and up the Seine toward the Canal du Loing.

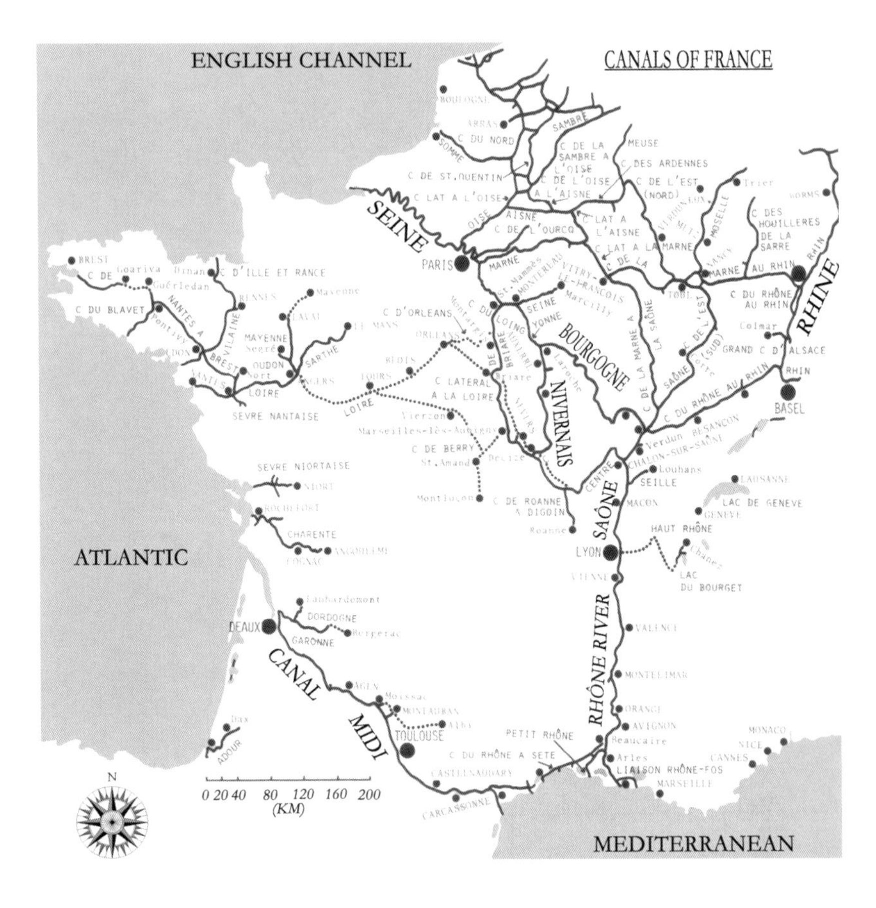

When we turn off the River Seine, the canal narrows to just 50 to 100 feet wide and locks are closer together. We maneuver ROCINANTE into locks only a few feet wider than her fender draped hull and tie off to bollards embedded in the top of the lock walls. The *eclusier*, the lockkeeper, operates the gates and sluices by hand to raise ROCINANTE about 15 feet to the level of the next section of the canal. In the 1800s, the size of the locks was standardized to fit commercial barges—called *peniches*—that were 38 meters long and 5 meters wide. Since World War II, trucks and trains have largely displaced peniches for hauling freight, but we've been told to watch out for the few that remain.

Views of the rural countryside from the canal are beautiful, with yellow rapeseed blooming and green wheat waving in the fields. Wildflowers bloom in profusion along the banks of the canal. It's still chilly in April but there's more sun and the promise of a warm spring. We're enjoying a leisurely pace.

We're approaching a lock whose gates are closed. With binoculars I can see the top part of a behemoth peniche in the lock, facing our way. We stop a few hundred feet before the lock. This is the first time we're faced with passing one of these monsters in a narrow canal and we want to give it plenty of room. The gates are opening. The black hulk is so loaded down its decks are almost awash. It's engine roars and diesel smoke billows into the air, as the peniche strains to gain headway. Its blunt bow pushes a wall of canal water in front of it. ROCINANTE sits dead in the water, as far over toward one bank as we can float. It looks like there will be just enough room for him to pass by. Just as its bow is passing our bow, water from the peniche's wake rushes along its hull, sucking us against its black steel side. I gun our engine but we have no way on and are pressed flat against the other hull, scraping down its side. One squashed white polyball fender, now being rubbed black, rolls between the hulls, saving ROCINANTE'S paint job. A woman throws open the peniche's wheelhouse door and runs along the deck, screaming at us in French, probably saying we are stupid Americans who

A peniche in the morning mist

have no business being here. The peniche, flying a Belgian flag, lumbers around a bend in the canal and out of sight. We sit, stunned, wondering what we should've done to avoid the near catastrophe. We could have tied off to a tree along the towpath, if the canal was deep enough to reach the bank. We could have kept moving as we passed the peniche, so that ROCINANTE'S momentum might keep her from being sucked against the peniche's hull. That seems like the best solution to try next time.

We can stop for the night anywhere the canal is deep enough at the bank to float ROCINANTE. We carry some heavy reinforcing steel bars to drive into the ground to tie off the boat. Along the way we found and liberated a 2 x 12 board to act as a walkplank to get from our deck to shore. Quaint little villages are spaced every few miles along the canal, where we can find baguettes and basic food, and can fill our jerry cans with diesel fuel and water.

In the town of Briare we're surprised to meet our Texas friends from the barge we were moored with all winter, VERTROUWEN. We're going in the same direction, so we decide to travel together through the locks. At Briare, the canal crosses the Loire River in the longest aqueduct in France—a mile-long, water-filled steel trough supported 100 feet above the river. We continue southeast into Burgundy, reaching the highest point of the canal on May 17.

Today, ROCINANTE'S tied up at a very nice marina in the sizable city of Chalon-sur-Saone. Mary must find a dentist. She had developed a bad toothache 3 months ago in Paris. A Parisian dentist, for a very cheap price and using tools passed down to him by his grandfather, had given Mary a reasonably pain-free root canal and installed a temporary cap, which he explained might fall off before we got home. It has, and a boat captain from the area is giving Mary the name of a local dentist. Using a town center map, we find the address and enter the crowded waiting room, where Mary tries her "mal de dent," pointing to the missing cap. The reply from behind the counter is a rapid string of sentences in uninterpretable French. After a long and awkward pause, Mary is handed a scrap of paper with a name and address. We find the new address, knock on the door and a woman in dental garb opens it. Mary starts to give her "mal de dent" spiel when the woman says "come on in" in perfect American English. The lady dentist was born in Chicago. She and her French dentist husband have lived and worked here for

Through the locks to the Med, 1993

many years. She says she'll make Mary a permanent cap. I guess, or rather hope, that a foreign sailor can find emergency medical or dental care in most any civilized country.

ROCINANTE hasn't been out of the water to have her bottom painted in over 2 years. Our friends recommend we detour up the River Saone to St.

Jean de Losne, where there is a boatyard with a crane capable of lifting ROCINANTE onto the shore. In late May, a hundred locks after leaving Paris, we arrive in St. Jean de Losne, an inland seaport where several canals intersect. Monsieur Blanquart, owner of the boatyard and operator of the boatyard's crane, says ROCINANTE weighs 17 tons and is his heaviest lift of the season. As we prepare to paint ROCINANTE'S bottom, we meet and get to know many other boat owners working on their boats, mostly Brits and Americans. An American lady from Hawaii, finding out my birthday is June 2, arranges a party at a local cafe and invites most of the English speaking community. It's an uproarious occasion, complete with inflatable cake and candles, one of my most memorable birthday celebrations, and hangovers. When ROCINANTE'S paint job is complete, we hate to leave St. Jean de Losne and can only hope we'll see our new friends again.

A heavy lift, St. Jean de Losne, France

We head down the River Saone and into the wide Rhone, stopping at cities and towns with medieval cathedrals, ancient stone walls and winding streets full of houses hundreds of years old—Chalon, Tournus, Lyon, Viviers, Avignon and Arles. The swift current is with us and, except for occasional strong winds from a mistral, the weather is warm and good. We arrive at the mouth of the Rhone, Port St. Louis, on July 2. A boatyard there is equipped with a crane to step ROCINANTE'S mast. We linger in a marina there, enjoying the warm Mediterranean sun and awaiting a favorable wind to sail across the Gulf of Lions to Cadaques, just over the French-Spanish border. On July 23 we make a 115 mile overnight sail and anchor in a rocky bay at Cadaques in northeast Spain.

Cadaques, a delightful village where Picasso and Salvador Dali once lived, is a resort catering to weekenders from Barcelona. A naked lady wades beside our anchorage, gathering sea urchins. However, when the wind picks up we drag anchor and have to hunt another spot. Many of the other boats have moved elsewhere, and we find them in a more protected cove. We anchor in the outermost part of the crowded cove, where the water is 70 feet deep. ROCINANTE'S anchor chain is only 200 feet long, too short for the textbook recommended scope of seven to one, but our 44-pound Bruce anchor holds us through the night.

From Cadaques we daysail to a marina near Barcelona, visit Barcelona by bus, and then sail overnight to anchor in the outer harbor of Mahon, Menorca, in the Balearic islands. Every morning two young men arrive in a skiff to deliver yesterday's weather forecast, collect our garbage and charge a small fee for anchoring. After a week we shift to a town mooring in Mahon's inner harbor. During Horatio Nelson's time, Mahon was headquarters for the entire British Mediterranean fleet. It's still a sailor's town, and the cosmopolitan capitol of the island. Each day at noon we relax in the shade of an awning outside our favorite restaurant and are served aperitifs and lunch by the same dignified Spanish waiter in a tuxedo. Yesterday, the king and queen of Spain passed by on their way to lunch.

This afternoon I dinghy ashore and start a long walk, while Mary remains on ROCINANTE to read and take a nap. Hours later, when I return to the dinghy and start toward our mooring, ROCINANTE isn't there. I frantically look across the harbor and finally spot ROCINANTE on another mooring. On board, Mary tells me how, soon after I had left, the wind picked up, there was a loud "pop" from the bow and the mooring ball float was no longer attached to the mooring. ROCINANTE drifted through the fleet of moored boats. Mary ran up from below, clad in her underwear, cranked the engine and coolly circled the harbor between the other boats until, finally, another sailor saw her predicament and helped her fasten on to an empty mooring. I think it's fantastic she handled it so well, by herself in her underwear.

A lazy summer day, Porto Colom

After 3 weeks of living in Mahon and exploring Menorca, we daysail to the island of Majorca and anchor in a bay off Porto Colom, a lazy fishing village on the opposite side of the island from the capital, Palma. Fishing boats line the commercial quay, and stretched out nets dry in the sun. We love the laid back innocence of this town, the old ladies playing cards at pine shaded sidewalk tables, the hot stillness of the streets and shuttered houses at siesta time and the friendly gatherings at a waterside cafe in the evenings. We intend to stay here until close to the time when Robert and Jamie are due to meet us in Alicante, on the mainland, only an overnight sail away. We move ROCINANTE into the tiny rickety Porto Colom marina, where a few other foreign sailors are settled in for the summer.

A few days, ago a local fishing boat sank offshore, and two fishermen were drowned. Now all of the other fishing boats have returned to the village and the quay is full, except for the one empty space, where the lost boat was always tied up. Posters with photographs and eulogies for the drowned men are pasted in windows all over the town. It's Sunday evening and, from ROCINANTE'S cockpit, I hear the slow hollow beat of a drum, from a hill where the church stands. A long procession of townspeople, led by a priest, is walking slowly down the winding road to the quay. They stand quietly together in front of the empty space where the drowned fishermen's boat used to be moored and each person, in turn, tosses a bouquet of flowers into the water. The space is full of the bright colors of floating flowers.

ANTONIA ANGEL, before she went down, Porto Colom harbor

We've met another American couple here. He sailed single-handed from Alaska to Australia, and she joined him there to continue around the world. They tried to sail to the Seychelle Islands and round the southern tip of Africa, but were forced by weather to land in India; they then continued through the Red Sea and Suez Canal to the Mediterranean and are now on their way to Gibraltar. We swap stories over pitchers of beer outside a local cafe and rent a car and explore Majorca together.

Robert and Jamie are due to meet us in Alicante on October 4, so we sail back to the mainland on September 29. We feel lucky that the boys are still available for the homeward leg across the Atlantic. They arrive a day late and we begin our journey along the Costa Brava and Costa del Sol, toward Gibraltar. Our first stop is an anchorage in front of the yacht club at Cartagena. An official at the yacht club says we can tie up at their pier but, he says, we may have trouble getting our anchor up. Sure enough, it takes a mud covered Spanish diver an hour to extricate ROCINANTE'S anchor and chain from a mass of sunken boats and machinery in front of the club. Our other stops before Gibraltar are a rough quay at Aguilas and a beautiful marina at Almunecar, where we rent a car to explore Granada and to provision for the Atlantic crossing.

ROCINANTE tied up at Marina Bay, Gibraltar, October 1993

Chapter 9

Heading Home

On October 21, ROCINANTE is tied up at Marina Bay, Gibraltar. We rendezvous with Phil and Jill on DELIVERANCE, who are heading east toward Turkey, and with our Alaskan friends, who are selling their boat here and flying home. We're casual about preparations for the relatively short run to the Canaries, a 450-mile warm-up for the 2800 mile tradewind passage to Barbados. We tour the island with our friends, feed the Barbary apes and wait for a favorable wind to clear the Straits of Gibraltar. On October 26, the wind blows fair from the east and there's no hint of bad weather pending, other than a weak depression way out to the west of Africa, shown at the very corner of a weather map in a Spanish newspaper. We fuel up and, accompanied by a brilliant half moon, motor sail across the Strait, past Tangier and toward a lighthouse marking the northwest tip of Africa.

Three days out and with little wind, we've had to motor part of each day to maintain progress of at least 4 knots toward the southwest. It's calm enough to spot whales blowing and diving a half mile off in the distance. Robert and Jamie are exuberant about being at sea again. Jamie says he could stay at the wheel for at least 2 days, without a break.

It's our fourth day out and the wind is freshening and beginning to head us. Mary picks up a weather forecast on Radio France International, warning of coup de vent, pending gales from the southwest, moving into our area. During the afternoon we reach the same latitude as Charleston, S.C., but we hesitate to celebrate. We're 60 miles off the coast of Morocco and almost half way to the island of Lanzarote, in the Canaries. As night falls, the southwest wind picks up to a steady 30 knots. Robert and Jamie reduce sail to a double reefed main and the staysail. We're beating as close as we can to the south southeast, but we won't be able to clear this bulge in the coast of Africa. With the wind still increasing, we decide to heave to, under the double reefed main and a storm jib. We turn on the spreader lights to give the boys more light to work the foredeck and remove the staysail. ROCINANTE'S bow won't stay up into the wind, so I start the engine to bring her up. A loose storm jib sheet washes overboard through a scupper and wraps around the prop. The engine stops dead. The boys manage to put up the storm jib.

It's dawn when Mary spots an Italian freighter, GIOVANNI GRAMALDI, close abeam. We call her on the VHF to get an up-to-date weather forecast. The Spanish forecast is for Force 5 to 6 in our area and 6 to 8 closer to the Canaries. They suggest we go in at the Moroccan port of Safi, 50 miles east of us. We have no chart of Safi but Reeds Almanac describes the approaches and harbor. We decide to go for Port Safi and we're able to make 4 knots in that direction. When we're about 30 miles off, I call Port Safi Radio and speak with a harbor official. I ask him the condition of the seas entering the harbor. I'm on standby while he looks. He returns to the radio and tells me there's a 4 to 5 meter (13 to 16 foot) swell entering the harbor. There's no way we can approach a harbor safely in those conditions, especially with no engine. Robert and Jamie confirm my feeling, that we'd end up on the rocks. Now, we're only 15 miles off Safi and need to heave to on the other tack to gain some sea room. We don't have enough speed to tack through the wind, so we head downwind to jibe to the other tack. With 30 knots of relative wind behind us, the main boom whips across with a bang and the mainsail splits a seam from leach to luff. The boys manage to get the flogging mainsail down and tied to the boom and boom gallows, and to raise the storm trysail.

Robert and Jamie steering in the gale

Now we're hove to in a full gale with 20-foot seas bashing into our port side. With our options running out, although we still haven't dragged a drogue or run under bare poles, and not knowing how much punishment ROCINANTE can take, I tell Mary and the boys it's time to put on our life-jackets. We'll know where they are, even if we don't have to use them. With the wheel tied hard over, hatches dogged down and companionway slats in place, we stand our watches, all through the night, from the bottom of the companionway steps. Every few minutes a big wave hits us broadside with a crash that's deafening. The hull shudders and dishes and glasses are rolled out of lockers and smashed on the cabin sole. Water is forced in around the forward hatch, around the anchor hawes hole and into the chain locker, and squirts up through the galley sink drain. Before I can close the galley sink seacock, the whole dining table is awash and the radio for receiving weather reports is soaked. Some of the time, the portholes on the port side are like looking into a washing machine window during the wash cycle. I look at Mary and the boys, as we brace ourselves against the table. We're all soaking wet, miserable and scared. To myself, I pray for our lives, and especially for our sons. Out of a porthole I can see the almost full moon casting an eerie glow on giant swells as they approach, plow under us and speed away toward the African coast.

Today, Halloween, the wind is between 35 and 45 knots, always from the southwest. We're being driven back toward Gibraltar. I copy our GPS position in the log every hour. We've been driven back 80 miles and are now closer to Portugal than the Canaries. I halfway joke with the boys about turning downwind, putting into Portugal and completing the voyage next year. We're able to joke a little now because we're convinced ROCINANTE can take a lot more punishment than we originally thought. The barometer has fallen 10 more millibars. Very heavy rains fall through most of Halloween night. Thunder rumbles and lightning streaks through the sky. One bolt of lightning is so bright I can see the moon backlit through the rain clouds.

Today the wind is beginning to let up.We've been hove to for 40 hours. We're able to tack back and forth with the trysail, storm jib and a little piece of jib, making up some of the lost miles. The boys take the mainsail off the boom and shove it below. In spite of miserable conditions and ROCINANTE'S rolling, Mary spends 4 hours handstitching and patching the rip in the sail. By nightfall it's back up, with a single reef and we're making 3 knots toward Lanzarote.

Stitching the ripped mainsail

It's November 2 and we're again opposite Charleston. This morning, while I was asleep, it was calm enough for Jamie to be let over the side to cut the line off the prop shaft. Now, we have the engine again. The wind is coming around to the west, blowing 20 to 25 knots, and we're able to use the windvane to steer a course toward the Canaries. It seems that the old sea bitch is going to let us through after all.

It's November 3, our eighth day out of Gibraltar, with 220 miles to go. The wind's backing again to the southwest and the barometer's falling. By early afternoon we're beating against 30 to 35 knots. The mainsail takes a sudden gust and splits all the way across along another seam. We heave to, again, with trysail, staysail and engine to hold us into the wind. It's late afternoon and raining very hard. I hold the wheel, hard over, giving the engine a little more throttle when the seas try to push the bow around. I'm soaked to the skin and convinced the sea wants us for a garden ornament. The sea's building again and I can imagine another night of hell and chaos. All of a sudden, the wind shifts ninety degrees and becomes even stronger than before. I hold on. Within an hour the wind velocity has dropped to 25 knots and is steady from the northwest. We roll out a little jib, set the windvane toward Lanzarote and begin to relax.

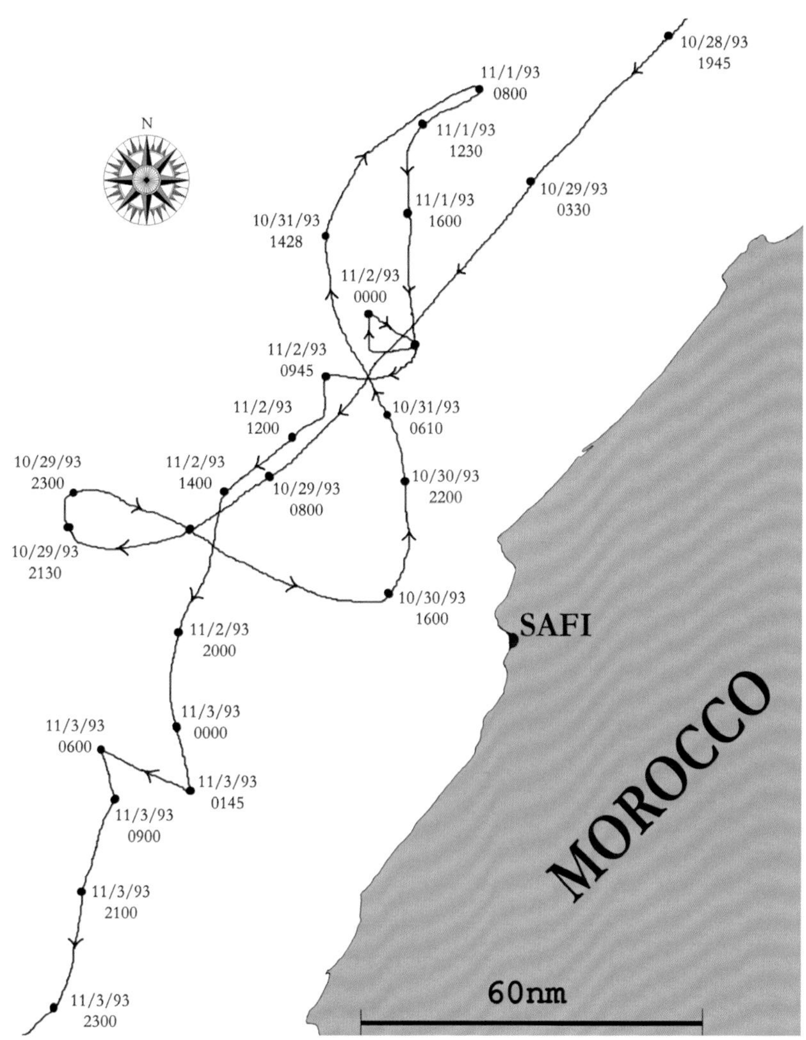

ROCINANTE's track during the gale

Today, November 5, while landing our first fish of the passage, a 15 pound dorado, Robert yells, "Land Ho." The black volcanic mountains of Lanzarote are in sight in the distance. By 2000, we're anchored outside the harbor of Puerto de Naos, near Arrecife, Lanzarote, Canary Islands, downwind of a sardine cannery. It's taken 11 days to make 650 miles. After an early dinner of baked dorado, we collapse in our bunks and sleep like stones.

Next morning, as we motor into the Puerto de Naos harbor a Brit shouts, "Well done" from the bow of his boat. Apparently we're the first boat to make it from Gibraltar since the gale ended. Later in the day, a 50-foot German sailboat, ERANOS, arrives. We had met her crew of attractive young men and women in Majorca. As together we celebrate being alive, they tell us about their storm experiences, of the staysail boom being ripped loose and sliding up the forestay where it whipped the mast and threatened to break their mainmast shrouds. Andrew, the captain, had to be hoisted up the mainmast in a bosun's chair to pull the heavy wooden staysail boom and the shredded sail back down to the deck.

ERANOS must have a replacement staysail and ROCINANTE a new main, so we order them together from a sailmaking company in England, which promises delivery to the airport at Grand Canary within 2 weeks. We've been unable to find any sailmaker on Lanzarote, other than a transplanted Arizona American who makes windsurfer sails and agrees to make temporary patches for our frayed jib and staysail. While waiting for sails to be repaired, we tour Lanzarote's black deserts, where vineyards grow out of holes dug in the black sand, and tourists ride across the dunes on camels. We eat at a restaurant where steaks are cooked over flames from a not quite dormant volcano. Robert and Jamie talk me into accompanying them and the crew of ERANOS on a night of partying with the kings of the windsurfing world and the queens of the Disco. Oh, for the energy of youth again.

Every boat in Puerto de Naos is making repairs and preparations for the tradewind crossing to the Caribbean. When I change the fuel filters for ROCINANTE'S engine, I find them almost completely clogged with reddish brown sediment, probably jostled off the bottom of the fuel tanks by the storm. I decide to clean the tanks before filling them with clean diesel. I pump the remaining fuel into buckets and dispose of it in the only place available, the sandy parking lot. I unbolt the inspection plate, reach down and feel an inch of oozy gunk on the bottom of the tank. It takes an hour of spooning out goo and wiping the inside with rags before the tank seems clean enough to use again. I suspect the diesel fuel at marinas in Spain, France, Ireland and England might not be as clean as American fuel, but I suppose it could happen at home, too.

After picking up the patched sails, we cruise south to the island of Fuerteventura, spend 2 nights there and make an overnight passage to Mogan on Grand Canary Island. Here, I buy a replacement SSB radio receiver for twice the price of the same model in the USA. Mogan Marina is completely full of boats, so we move to a slip at Puerto Rico Marina to wait for our new mainsail. On November 23, Andrew of ERANOS and I hire a cab to the airport to pick up our new sails. It takes almost all of a frustrating day to get them through Customs and back to the marina. The sail slides for the boom track are the wrong size and we have to substitute ones from the old sail. Finally, we raise the new $1400 sail to the top of the mast. The goddamned thing is too big. There's still eighteen inches of sailcloth bagged out at the bottom. At first I think I put the wrong dimensions on the faxed drawing I sent them to make the sail, but we spread the sail out in the parking lot, measure it and find they just made it too big. I telephone England and raise hell with a haughty Englishman, who finally admits their mistake, something about a sailmaker with dyslexia transposing the dimensions. He offers to deliver another sail within 3 weeks. By now, I've lost it. We can't wait 3 more weeks—we're already late to start across the Atlantic. I tell the guy we'll have to put a reef in his sail to use it, but we'll get home somehow, and that he better have me a new sail back in South Carolina when we get there. He agrees.

ERANOS prepares to leave for Antigua a day before we're scheduled to leave for Barbados. We see them off, comforting the sniffling mother of one of the crew, who has flown over from Germany to see her son embark onto the big dangerous ocean. I know Andrew is nervous, when he starts to pump diesel fuel into the waste holding tank instead of the fuel tank. Robert and one of the ERANOS girls have a thing going, which they promise to renew when ROCINANTE gets to Antigua. We watch the Germans disappear into the sunset.

We get underway on November 26, sailing down the coast of Africa toward the Cape Verde Islands, hoping to catch the trades at about 25-25—latitude 25 degrees north, longitude 25 degrees west—and turn downwind toward the west. We each write down our predicted arrival time in Barbados, the one closest to actual time to be declared winner. The weather is almost perfect. We have an easy reach, making an average of 140 miles a day for the first 3 days, fast for a heavy displacement 38-footer, with a baggy reefed main. During the second day, we cross the Tropic of Cancer and, that night are treated to the sight of an eclipse of the full moon.

We stay on a reach until about 21-21, or about 200 miles north of the Cape Verde's, when we pick up the trades and turn downwind. ROCINANTE has no spinnaker, so the reefed mainsail is vanged out to one side of the mast and the genoa poled out to the other, wing and wing. The winds are strong enough to operate the windvane steering. The constant rolling from side to side begins, 15 degrees to starboard, then 15 degrees to port, thirteen times a minute, as regular as clockwork. I calculate we'll roll 300,000 or 400,000 times before we reach Barbados. We have to get used to living with it, walking with it, sleeping with it, eating with it—it won't go away.

A haircut on the foredeck, wing on wing to Barbados

Jamie catches dinner in the Trades

We're catching fish every day, dorado, bull dolphin, some over 15 pounds. Robert and Jamie set out as many as four handlines, trailing green or yellow feather lures from steel leaders, 100 to 200 feet behind ROCINANTE. The other end of the 100-pound test line is wrapped on a spool and tied off to a cleat or a winch, with a clothes pin clipped to the fishing line and a lifeline, which snaps off when the fish strikes. Since we're making more than 6 knots and don't want to slow down, the fish puts a big drag on the line when he hits. A big one's hard to pull in, hand over hand with the gloves, until he's close enough to the stern to gaff and land on deck. The fish's bright blue and green colors fade right away once he's out of the water. Robert or Jamie holds him down on the deck with his knee and butchers him right away, stowing the fillets below for dinner and cleaning the blood off the deck with buckets of salt water. We only keep what we can eat and we eat their delicious meat at least once every day, fixed in every conceivable way. We never suffer from lack of good food. Mary is even baking her own bread.

We listen every morning to Trudy's Net, regular SSB radio conversations between sailboats making the tradewind crossing and Trudy, who is stationed in Barbados and dedicated to helping sailors with their problems. A lot of the conversations are trivial gossip but she does provide an important service. The weather has been kind to us for this crossing, 20 to 25 knots of steady breeze out of the east. We listen to one sailor, whose rudder has broken loose. Every other sailor seems to have a different solution to his problem. Each morning he reports his progress in trying to fix it. He apparently has a welding machine on board and is finally able to make a repair and put the whole thing back in working order.

Two weeks out and we're averaging better than 6 knots. Mary and I celebrate our thirty-third wedding anniversary. We rarely touch the wheel, only occasionally jibing to the other tack to correct our heading. We stand our watches, fish and read. We've been in sight of only one other boat since the first day. Caribbean music on the radio now, no more African music. Soon after midnight, on December 16, we spot the lights of Barbados. We tie up to the Customs pier at Bridgetown the next morning, 19 days and 14 hours out of Grand Canary, a fine passage.

There's no marina for tying up in Bridgetown. We anchor off a broken down pier and, to get ashore, ride the dinghy through the swells to the end of the pier. Occasionally, we make a much longer dinghy trip into Bridgetown to shop. We make a visit to the Mt. Gay Rum Center, but it's cheaper to buy rum in the supermarket at $2 a liter. Everyone seems friendly and helpful in Barbados. Many of the ancestors of African Americans in South Carolina were brought as slaves from Africa to Barbados, before they were sold to South Carolina planters to work in the rice fields.

After a week in Barbados, we make a 100 mile passage to Bequia. Among the many sailboats here are several Scandinavian ones, anchored in Admiralty Bay for the Christmas holidays. All of the boats use the Frangipani Hotel dinghy dock. Robert, Jamie and I are walking along the beach to an open air market, where we're supposed to replenish ROCINANTE'S fresh vegetable supply. The market is operated by three Rastafarians, who talk nonstop, filling orders and collecting money from mostly local shoppers. They talk so fast it's hard to understand what they're saying. I point at a pile of tomatoes and a Rasta grabs three or four and puts them on the table, talking all the time, saying "You need some tomatoes, you need some potatoes," grabbing four or six potatoes, saying, "You need some peppers, you need some onions," grabbing them for the pile, until there's a big stack of vegetables on the table in front of me. It's possible we could use everything he's piled up, so I ask him the price. The Rastas confer. "Mon, one hundred twenty dollars is all you need". I tell him I can't pay that much. He begins to put things back, talking all the time, saying, "You don't need so much potatoes, but you need some potatoes. You need some tomatoes but you don't need so many peppers." The pile dwindles to a much smaller size. How much, I ask. "Mon, fifty five dollars, that's all you need." I pay. "I throw in the bag," he flashes a gaptooth smile. I know I've been had, but I smile too.

New Year's Day, 1994, is celebrated in front of the Frangipani Hotel with a big barbecue, and all of the boats fire off their out of date flares. We enjoy revisiting many of the places on the island we first saw in 1988. Jamie and I cross over to Moon Hole, a bizarre vacation community of rich Americans and Europeans, who live in weird rustic stone and concrete homes, all designed by the same New York architect-developer. On the way back to ROCINANTE we stop at the whaling museum, where an old black man describes how the natives continue to catch a few whales, harpooning them from open dories. Just before we leave Bequia I buy a model of a sailing whaleboat from the excellent model shop.

From Bequia, we sail north to the Pitons, on St. Lucia, where we are moored between a buoy and an almond tree. The Pitons are two steep volcanic cones that can be seen from far offshore. We revisit Marigot Bay and Rodney Bay, before anchoring off St. Pierre, Martinique, a town that was completely destroyed by a volcanic eruption of Mt. Pelee in 1902. Robert and Jamie must climb Mt. Pelee before we move on. Next, we anchor off Roseau, Dominica, and they climb Trafalgar Falls. We spend another night anchored at Îles des Saintes, before reaching over to English Harbor, Antigua.

We anchor in the congested but pleasant outer harbor, fringed by reefs and a sandy beach at the base of a high cliff, where we await a rendezvous with ERANOS and Robert's German girlfriend. Every morning an attractive British woman from a nearby sailboat swims past ROCINANTE, doing a slow breaststroke and singing the same song, Gershwin's Ain't Misbehavin', in time to her stroke. Midway through our third day here, a Swedish sailboat motors through the entrance and anchors between us and the beach, letting out two anchors to keep his boat from swinging into shallow water. Every other boat here is swinging on one anchor. I can see there's going to be trouble because, when the tide changes ROCINANTE and the other boats will swing around but the Swedish boat won't. Sure enough, as ROCINANTE swings, the Swedish captain and I watch each other getting closer and closer together. He tells me I should put out a second anchor or shorten up on my chain to keep from hitting him. I explain that we can't put out two anchors because the other boats will swing into us, that we have out just enough chain to keep from dragging and that we were here first. He declares that I'm uncooperative. I tell him we're in the right and, if he doesn't think so he can hire a lawyer, the American way. "No lawyers," he screams, becoming red in the face. He storms below, reappears with an unhappy blonde mate, ups anchor and motors away.

After a week we shift from the outer to the inner harbor, anchoring next to mangroves that screen the backyards of houses lining the shore. I hear the sound of a lawn mower and am startled to catch glimpses of a nude woman pushing her mower back and forth past a break in the mangroves. Later, ashore, Robert and I do a little archeological poking around the site of a new sewage treatment plant and find a few artifacts from a time when Admiral Nelson was commander of the British base here. Other than the quaintness of English Harbor, Antigua is an expensive cruise ship tourist trap. We've been here long enough to do all there is to do. The crews of the rich charter yachts that winter here must have a hard time fighting off alcoholism, what with the cheap rum and frequent Happy Hours.

ROCINANTE anchored off the Pitons, St. Lucia

When ERANOS finally returns to English Harbor, Robert discovers his German girlfriend has fallen for another member of the ERANOS crew. In disgust, Robert decides to fly back to South Carolina and start something new. Jamie says he'll remain with us until we get to the Virgin Islands. I'm beginning to get a little antsy to get home. I'm not sure what I'll do when we get there, but all during the trip, and especially in France, we've been working on dream house plans, and even a cardboard model of our own French farmhouse, to be built somewhere in America. We get underway on January 24, stopping only once, in Nevis, before tying up at a marina in Red Hook, St. Thomas.

Mary's brother, Ned, arrives a few days later to spend a week on ROCINANTE. He's an Episcopal minister, a former Naval person and good company to have on board. We make the rounds of the U.S. and British Virgins, stopping overnight at St. John, Cooper Island, Sopers Hole and Jost Van Dyke, before returning to Red Hook. The day after Ned flies home to Jacksonville, Jamie, who is obviously feeling homesick, returns to South Carolina to cement a serious relationship and find a new job.

Mary and I are alone on ROCINANTE again, for the first time since last October. We spend another 5 weeks in the Virgin Islands, mostly at Red Hook and Coral Bay on St. John, because it's still too early in the season to sail much further north. We renew our friendship with an American sailing couple we first met in Falmouth in 1991. Don and Sandy have lived, full time, on their 41-foot Morgan sloop, MISTICK, for 15 years. They're cruising north to Florida and we decide to travel together for part of the way. We leave Red Hook on March 19, on a short passage to Culebra. We anchor in Ensanada Honda, which was devastated by a hurricane 2 years ago. Boat wreckage still litters the shore. A young uniformed female Customs agent, who is all business, clears us through U.S. Customs. This same lady turns up again that evening, transformed into a carefree, sexy waitress at the local cantina.

We sail along the south coast of Puerto Rico, anchoring for a night at Palmas del Mar and then Salinas. There are twenty or thirty sailboats anchored on one side of a wide bay, near the small pleasant village of Salinas. Across the bay is a restaurant and a ramp for launching boats from trailers. It's Saturday morning and lots of speedboats are being launched. They're roaring up and down the bay. We've just tied the dinghy alongside ROCINANTE, after a shopping trip to town, and are sitting in the cockpit sipping a cold beer. Mary goes below to fix lunch. She tells me to come down to the main cabin, where it's not so hot and a cool breeze is blowing through the open portholes. I'm just about to take the first bite out of a sandwich, when I hear the high pitched whine of an outboard engine, coming closer and getting louder, very fast. In a split second there's a deafening crash that shakes ROCINANTE like the biggest breaking wave in the Atlantic. One of the companionway doors flies across the cockpit and splinters against a bulkhead. I'm looking out of the companionway at bits of red fiberglass scattered all over the deck. Mary screams and sits frozen. I finally find the courage to climb the companionway steps. The remains of a red speedboat with a big outboard engine is floating alongside us, beginning to fill with water. The bow is gone, disintegrated into a thousand pieces of fiberglass. There's no one in the boat or in the water. I'm looking for blood or bubbles or some sign of life.

Damage from the speedboat crash, Salinas, Puerto Rico

Now other motorboats are alongside the speedboat. Someone finds the driver, wedged under the dashboard of the speedboat. He may be alive. They transfer the unconscious young man to another boat and take him back to the ramp. An ambulance speeds away. Other boats tow the sinking speedboat back to the landing. It's all done in Spanish. I don't remember anyone asking me anything in English.

ROCINANTE is a mess. First, the speedboat had hit the side of our rubber dinghy, destroying it and the engine, and flipping the speedboat up, probably saving the man's life. The speedboat then catapulted through ROCINANTE'S caprail and lifelines, before smashing into the solid aft corner of the trunk cabin, stopping dead and sliding back into the water. Our friend, Don, from MISTICK, rows his dinghy over to us. He saw the whole episode from his cockpit. He says the boat had been speeding back and forth on the other side of the bay, probably practicing for Sunday's speedboat race. The boat had the name of the restaurant painted on its sides. It made a turn at more than 60 miles an hour, lost control and headed for the sailboat anchorage. If he hadn't hit ROCINANTE, he would have hit the next boat. Don rows us ashore, so we can inquire about the driver of the boat. The police are there and say he is in intensive care. We ask who owns the boat and does he have insurance. A policeman talks with several people in Spanish. After a few minutes, a man in a dirty white kitchen uniform stands by the policeman, who says, "He owns the boat. He has no insurance. He only speaks Spanish." We can see we'll learn no more and return to ROCINANTE.

A dinghy pulls alongside ROCINANTE. An American with a Southern accent offers me his services. Neil hands me a card, saying he's a marine surveyor. He explains that he and his family live on their sailboat and are headed for the Virgin Islands to start a marine surveying business there. I gratefully accept his offer. He does a thorough survey, and his wife types a report, complete with polaroid photographs of the damage. I've already called my insurance company, who contact their agent in San Juan. The agent drives to Salinas, accepts the report and authorizes me to proceed with the necessary temporary repairs to get back home. We ride over to the restaurant, where the wrecked boat is covered up, behind a fence. I ask him if the insurance company will try to collect from the owner of the restaurant. He says no, the owner is too powerful in this part of the country. They will write off the loss. I ask about the driver of the boat. He's the 20-year-old son of the restaurant owner. He's out of intensive care and will be scarred, but all right.

Neil offers to make the temporary repairs to ROCINANTE. He has a portable bandsaw and other power tools on board his boat, and a friend will help him. Within a few days ROCINANTE has lifelines, a treated pine caprail and a new engine for the destroyed dinghy, which we manage to inflate, despite it being declared a total loss. Don and Sandy, from MISTICK, wait for us to complete the repairs and we get underway again, after 2 weeks in Salinas. In spite of the accident we grew to like the place.

ROCINANTE and MISTICK continue along the south coast of Puerto Rico, stopping at Ensenada and Boqueron, before making a 3-day passage to the Caicos Islands. We're resting in an anchorage off Cockburn, South Caicos. Don and Sandy row over to ROCINANTE in their prized little dinghy, TIGER, which has survived almost 20 years of continuous service. I tie TIGER to a stanchion and we all sit below, having our evening cocktails and discussing the passage. Thirty minutes later Don and Sandy come up on deck to go back to MISTICK, and TIGER is gone. The tide's running out, it's almost dark and I must have done a poor job of tying her off. Don and I jump in ROCINANTE'S dinghy and I give the engine full throttle. I'm feeling terrible because I know I've lost her. Just at dark Don tells me it's no use and to turn around and start back. I throttle back, take one last look around and there she is, way out to one side, bobbing along. Don's like a kid who has just recovered his favorite toy. We grab TIGER'S painter and tow her back. What a relief.

The next day, we cross the Caicos Bank to Providenciales to reprovision. Alongside the town wharf, a battered derelict Haitian sailboat has unloaded a cargo of coconuts and is getting ready to leave. It has no engine. The crew raises its mainsail, sewn together from strips of faded cloth and the patched remains of a street banner advertising Shell Oil. They're underway in the fading light, bailing with buckets as they sail across the Bank, headed back toward Haiti.

The next morning we continue north, anchoring for a night in Abraham Bay, a rough and shallow place, off the island of Mayaguana, in the southern Bahamas. After a bouncy night, Don, as usual, is out on the foredeck of MISTICK before daylight, cranking on his anchor windlass, ready to get underway. Both sailboats touch a coral head before we're clear of Abraham Bay, glad to be out of there. We stop three more times; at the mosquito infested paradise of Atwood Harbor off Acklin Island; at Clarencetown, Long Island; and at Rum Cay, before reaching Georgetown, Exuma Island. We stay for a few days to watch the Out Island Regatta. MISTICK will take a different route from us, on her way to the west coast of Florida.

We sail alone toward Man-O-War Cay, stopping once to anchor off Little San Salvador. Today is warm and calm. Mary has the watch but there is nothing to see. The diesel pushes us along at 5 knots, guided by the autopilot. I lie face down on the bowsprit staring past patches of yellow Gulf weed into the dark blue depths and watching three porpoises lazily crossing back and forth under the bobstay. Mary is below, maybe sleeping on watch. I sit up, retrieve the handheld VHF and turn it to Channel 16. Disguising my voice, I transmit, "This is supertanker Mobil King crossing your bow. I suggest you take immediate evasive action to avoid imminent collision." Mary bolts out of the cabin desperately trying to disengage the autopilot and searching for the tanker. I howl and she lets me have a few choice words. Late that afternoon we arrive at the north Man-O-War channel in a violent lightning storm, waiting for a break to enter the channel and anchor off the marina. We stay at Man-O-War long enough to collect a trunk full of personal stuff from Pirates Den; then, sail directly for Charleston. ROCINANTE makes a slow passage and we arrive home exactly 3 years from the day we left. The entire voyage covered 13,000 miles.

One of my first orders of business is to check on the new mainsail from England. It hasn't come. I fax the sail company, offering to return the used sail and asking when the new one will be delivered. No reply. I repeat the fax, twice more. No reply. I see they're not planning to make good on their promise. I write a sailing article for a fictitious magazine, describing how much we enjoyed England, except for the unfortunate experience with the sail, naming the company. I send a fax, with a copy of the article to the company, saying I intend to have it published in several American and English sailing magazines. Early the next morning, an extremely polite official from the sail company calls me, saying that $1400 has been deposited in my bank, and I should keep the used sail and, is there anything else they can do?

Chapter 10

A Wedding on Vertrouwen

Mary and I have decided to find a lot and build the French farmhouse we have already designed. We agree we can't afford to keep ROCINANTE. She's fitted out to be a long distance cruising sailboat, and we don't intend to do any serious cruising for awhile. ROCINANTE'S permanent repairs from the speedboat crash, including another brand new paint job, are complete. I place a "For Sale" ad in *Soundings* magazine. When I buy the next issue, to make sure the ad is there, I notice a sketched profile of a Dutch barge for sale. It looks familiar and the ad lists a Texas telephone number. It must be VERTROUWEN, the barge we were rafted against in Paris. I show the ad to Mary. We talk about how much we enjoyed the canals and how much we're going to miss not having a boat. We decide it would be practical to buy VERTROUWEN, if we had a partner to share the cost and expenses. We talk with friends in Chapel Hill, North Carolina, and they think it would be a great idea to own a barge with us. In December, 1994, we buy VERTROUWEN and sell ROCINANTE.

ROCINANTE'S new owners are a folk-singing, blues-playing couple who plan to live aboard and make their living entertaining in the Caribbean. Robert and a friend help them sail ROCINANTE from Charleston to Pensacola, Florida. Mary and I watch sadly from the beach as ROCINANTE'S new tanbark mainsail disappears over the horizon.

We're living in a small house in Mt. Pleasant that we had bought as an investment years ago, where our furniture has been stored for 3 years, and we're beginning to believe we'll be using it as a base for awhile. Mary is starting to develop and print many of the black and white photographs she took in Europe, using the new darkroom I've built for her. I'm doing part-time work as a construction consultant but can't take on anything permanent, because we're scheduled to meet Bill and Frances, owners of VERTROUWEN, in France in April, 1995, to take possession of the barge. Before we leave for France, Jamie and Leigh announce they're going to be married in the summer. Both families think it would be a great idea for the ceremony to take place in France, on VERTROUWEN.

Motorship VERTROUWEN in profile

There are four of us—Bill and Frances and Mary and I—with all of our baggage, riding in a tiny French rental car from Paris to Burgundy, where the barge is moored. It's like a circus act, with me stuffed in last, riding for three and a half hours, lying on top of the others, with my head on the rear shelf, staring at the ceiling, and my feet on the dashboard. We finally reach the marina basin at St. Symphorien-sur-Saone, close to the place where we painted ROCINANTE'S bottom in 1993. We've seen the inside of VERTROUWEN only once, 2 years ago, and don't remember the details. We bought her without a survey, based on the meticulous care I watched Bill give her during our winter in Paris. She's a beautiful little barge, 48 feet long, small compared to many of the pleasure boats we saw on the canals. Her name means "Trustworthy" in Dutch. She was built of riveted iron in Holland in 1907 as a commercial sailing vessel. A family must have lived in the stern, with the middle part being the cargo hold. She was converted to a pleasure barge sometime in the 1960's, and a Perkins diesel installed in a compartment under the cockpit. Varnished oak leeboards still hang from both sides of the hull, once acting as keels when the shallow draft vessel sailed in the Iselmeer, but the mast and other rigging were removed long ago. Her original traditional anchor windlass remains

VERTROUWEN's nameboard

on the bow. She's steered from the aft cockpit by the original heavy oak tiller, fastened to a massive barn door rudder. Mahogany trim boards with incised carvings decorate the caprails.

To go below, I turn a big iron skeleton key in the brass lock of a heavy glass paned oak door and walk down three steps, from the cockpit into the main cabin. Everything down here is relatively modern, a nice galley with propane stove, small propane and electric refrigerator, propane instantaneous hot water heater, kitchen sink, ceramic tile top and adequate cabinet space. Forward of the galley the curved ceiling becomes progressively lower. Under a big skylight is the dining table and built-in seats, which convert into a second bedroom. The starboard side of the main cabin is lined with storage cabinets. Forward of the main cabin is the head, with a marine toilet and tiny fiberglass bathtub with a telephone shower. There's a hanging locker to starboard. The main sleeping quarters, with a pair of single beds, is far forward, where the headroom is only about five feet.

One of the things we love most about VERTROUWEN is the amount of light and ventilation below. There are two opening skylights in the forward bedroom and a big glass doghouse skylight in the main cabin. The eight opening portholes on each side of the trunk cabin were probably salvaged from a ship. The entire aft end of the galley is a wall of glass panes. The cockpit is covered by a canvas awning with side curtains that zip down to create another enclosed room.

VERTROUWEN's main cabin

Bill and Frances introduce us to their Australian friends, John and Ienka, who live on a nearby barge, ABSOLUUT. They remove their personal gear from VERTROUWEN and depart. We move on board and begin learning the idiosyncrasies of VERTROUWEN. Almost all of the necessary dishes, linens and tools have been left for us. We borrow the marina automobile from Roger, the dour Yorkshire owner of the marina, to provision in St. Jean de Losne, two kilometers away.

St. Symphorien marina is really just two wide basins, separated by a lock, along the Rhine-Rhone Canal, where twenty or thirty boats can raft up to the bank, three deep. The lower basin connects to the River Saone by another lock. The buildings and machinery from an abandoned water-powered grinding mill remain on the site. The marina setting is beautifully rural, with Charolais cattle grazing in grassy pastures and fields of rapeseed, wheat, and sunflowers all around.

Roger provides *gardiennage*, security, for the barges left here for the winter. Barges are owned by English, Swiss, Dutch, Belgians, Americans and others, who are now beginning to arrive and prepare for the coming season. They will scatter out onto the more than 5000 miles of French canals, and some will return in the fall. Only a few people live on their boats here during the winter.

John and Ienka are very helpful. John gives me my first lesson in handling VERTROUWEN. The little 50 horsepower diesel is the same model as the one in our sailboat, ATHENA. The biggest difference between operating VERTROUWEN and a sailboat is the flat bottom, which makes VERTROUWEN slide around corners. I have to get used to turning more sharply, to keep from sliding into the canal banks. I haven't steered with a tiller since MATRIARCH in 1976, and that takes some getting used to. Also, there's the bowthruster, a reversible electric motor, fitted into the bow. By operating a switch from the cockpit, I can shift our heading a little, making it easier to get lined up to enter a lock. VERTROUWEN has about the same beam as ROCINANTE, but the leeboards and leeboard winches protrude from the hull, making it more difficult to avoid hitting the sides of a lock. We hang enough fenders and polyballs over the side to minimize damage to the meticulously painted green and cream yellow hull. We make short maiden voyages to the nearby towns of Dole, Auxonne and St. Jean de Losne, becoming accustomed to VERTROUWEN. As we did on ROCINANTE, Mary handles the lines and climbs the ladders, and I steer. It doesn't take long to feel confident we can handle her. With only a 2-foot draft, she'll go almost anywhere.

We pick out a spot under the poplars along the towpath of the Rhine-Rhone Canal to hold the wedding ceremony on July 1. Our sons and Leigh's family arrive a few days early. The weather's so warm that Leigh and her sister, Molly, and the boys go swimming in the mill pond. Our barge partners, Hank and Martha, arrive and see VERTROUWEN for the first time. They move aboard. Martha, an irreverently outspoken ex-nun, will conduct the wedding ceremony. Mary has arranged for a French wedding cake called "pièce montée" (mountain of balls), elaborate hors d'oeuvres and an accordionist and a guitar-playing singer for the reception. We've collected and stored a large quantity of good but cheap champagne and Côtes du Rhone under our beds.

We're up early to prepare for the big event. Michelle, from the St. Jean de Losne Chamber of Commerce, arrives with ten kilos of hard-to-find ice, to chill

Here comes the bride!

Croquembouche and hors d'oeuvres in the cockpit

champagne in the bathtub. Except for Jamie and Martha, the wedding party gets underway aboard VERTROUWEN, decorated with wildflowers. Soon we arrive at the shady spot along the towpath where the ceremony is to take place. Leigh's sister, the Maid of Honor, adjusts the beautiful bride's gown and veil, as the ushers drive stakes and tie VERTROUWEN to the bank. The wedding party teeters down the walkplank, accompanied by the Wedding March from our CD player. Jamie and Leigh stand together on the towpath as Martha starts the ceremony. The bride and groom kiss, champagne toasts begin, many photos are taken and we begin the short journey back toward the marina.

Before the wedding reception, Bourgogne Marine, St. Symphorien

We approach a mown grassy bank where a tent has been set up, and the old accordionist plays traditional French ballads. We've invited the crews of all the boats in the marina to attend the reception. The party becomes much less formal as wine flows and dancing begins. However, heavy clouds are gathering, threatening rain. The bride and groom escape just as the bottom falls out. The tent is much too small to hold the crowd, so thirty celebrants jamb themselves inside of VERTROUWEN, to continue drinking wine and eating the last of the hors d'oeuvres and wedding cake, also known as "croquembouche" (crunch in the mouth). When all the food and wine are gone, the guests leave and we start a grand clean-up. Tomorrow, we're scheduled to participate in the Grand Pardon, a boat parade and blessing of the fleet in St. Jean de Losne.

VERTROUWEN is 2 hours late for the official parade, because of hangovers and other delays, but I know she would have won the prize for the most beautiful boat. She is decked out with balloons and paper flowers from the Chamber of Commerce, plus all of the courtesy flags from countries we visited on ROCINANTE, and wildflowers from the wedding. What's left of the wedding party takes part in the day's festivities, featuring a 20-foot inflated champagne bottle towed behind a barge, and hundred foot long commercial peniches driven wildly in circles by their inebriated captains. After a full day of celebration, we raft outside two larger barges for the night.

VERTROUWEN at the Grand Pardon, St. Jean de Losne, 1995

Everyone from the wedding party has returned to South Carolina except our partners. We're traveling along the Rhine-Rhone Canal, headed toward the Rhine River. We enter the Grand Canal Alsace, part of the canalized but swiftly flowing Rhine River, fortunately headed downstream. Across the river is Basel, Switzerland. A 3-knot current pushes us north. Giant freighters and hotel boats pass by, pulling wakes that rock VERTROUWEN and bounce off concrete banks to rock us again. After a night tied to a bollard large enough to hold a Rhine steamer, we're glad to turn off the river into a small canal and head toward our destination, Strasbourg.

The approach to Strasbourg is tranquil and pastoral, until we pass through a lock a few kilometers outside the city center. Suddenly, a 4-knot

Lunch along the River Doubs, Rhone au Rhine Canal

current is sweeping us forward. We check the chart book to make sure we haven't taken a wrong turn. The chart indicates a restricted channel ahead, just before a bridge that we must pass under. We round a curve and, just ahead is a solid three story building built across the entire canal, except for three little arched openings under the building, where canal water surges through at a tremendous rate. The chart shows the channel passing through the arch on the far side of the canal. We look for a place to tie up but the banks are steep and a commercial peniche is tied up to the only wall. I turn VERTROUWEN around just before the bridge and we barely hold our own against the current. We can't go back and it's going to be a tough job going forward. My partner, Hank, picks up a stout boat hook and says he'll fend off, as we go under the bridge. I tell him he's crazy because our weight and momentum would drive the boat hook through his stomach. I guess we've got to make a try. I tell everybody to hold on, and begin to turn VERTROUWEN downstream. I give her plenty of gas to get to the other bank before straightening up. We're headed for the opening and we're fairly straight. We might make it. Now, we're angling off, and there's nothing I can do about it. VERTROUWEN'S bow shoots under the arch but she's not straight, and she slams into the solid sandstone wall. The impact straightens us up and we shoot through and out the other side. The impact knocks Hank off his feet and he falls backwards, bouncing his head off the teak cockpit grating. He lies still. I call Martha to come see about him, because I can't leave the helm. We're still rocketing ahead and I see a bateau mouche loaded with passengers, churning upstream, toward us. We've barely got steerage, and we scrape by the bateau mouche as delighted passengers scream and point. Hank's getting up and says he's okay. Martha shouts back that there's another bridge ahead that's way too low for us to get under. I head for the closest bank and turn against the current. Mary throws a line over a bollard on the shore and we stop and tie up.

It takes awhile to regroup. There's no serious damage to VERTROUWEN, only a deep scratch in a leeboard and some particles of sandstone embedded in our paint job. We're right in the middle of Strasbourg, "La Petite France," surrounded by restaurants, shops and apartments. A man leans out of a window and tells Mary to walk around the next bend to a lock, where the eclusier will open the drawbridge and let us through the lock. After we pass the drawbridge and lock, we continue at high speed, looking for a place to tie up for the night. Excursion boats and peniches crowd the few quays available. We pass under several fixed arched bridges, so low that Mary has to hurriedly remove the radio antenna and the French courtesy flag. We pass Strasbourg cathedral and other big buildings without finding a landing place. We pass through another lock, and into the Marne au Rhin canal. The water is as placid as it was on the other side of Strasbourg. We're 2 miles past Strasbourg before we find a place to tie up alongside the towpath.

A Dutch cruiser is tied up behind us. As I'm touching up a few dings in the topside paint and thinking we should have backed under the stone arch, two men from the Dutch boat start to examine VERTROUWEN and discuss her in Dutch. The younger man tells me his father, who speaks only Dutch, was born on a sailing tjalk just like VERTROUWEN. He was one of ten children who lived aboard as they sailed her and hauled freight on the Iselmeer. The old man points out where the mast and rigging would have been and where the sleeping quarters and the coal fired stove were located. His boat had no engine and they often pulled their barge along the canal towpaths with ropes. In the center freight hold they carried potatoes and vegetables from farms in the country to the cities. His story makes me wonder who, exactly, owned VERTROUWEN and what she was doing before and after the times of World Wars I and II. I don't really know any way of finding out. I know she was built near Groningen, but her original hull markings are gone. Some day I'd like to cruise to northern Holland and find out if anyone recognizes her.

We take a bus into Strasbourg to tour the city. We're sitting outside a restaurant in La Petite France, where we can see the bridge we hit. The Michelin Guide says it's the Vauban Barrage, a fortified bridge built by Louis XIV's famous military engineer in the 17th century. One of its arches is now minus a few flakes of sandstone.

From Strasbourg we cruise along the Marne au Rhine canal, following a rural valley with steep evergreen forested hills on both sides. As we approach the town of Lutzelbourg, a fast train roars alongside the canal, squealing its airhorn. There's immediate silence as the train disappears into a tunnel through the mountain. At Lutzelbourg we're delayed by repairs being made to one of the locks. I walk ahead and watch workmen drill down through 150-year-old blocks of stone to install steel bars and concrete to strengthen the lock walls. It must be extremely expensive for the French government to maintain and operate the locks and canal systems. We paid a fee of about $300 to use all French canals for a whole season. Maybe hireboat companies and hotel boats pay more, but I bet it's a losing proposition for the Government.

After Lutzelbourg, we encounter one of the wonders of the French canal system, the inclined plane. VERTROUWEN is tied up in a pond at the bottom of a 200-foot cliff. The canal stops here and starts up again at the top of the cliff. To get from here to there, the French built a steep concrete ramp and a set of cables and counterweights, which transports a gigantic steel tub on rollers, up and down the ramp. A door in the end of the underwater tub opens and VERTROUWEN enters. The door closes, sealing the tub, and electric motors attached to cables pull the tub out of the basin and slowly up the ramp. Halfway up, concrete block counterweights on the other end of the cables pass under our tub. At the top, 200 feet above the pond, we stop, the door opens and VERTROUWEN motors out into the canal. Without the inclined plane it would take ten or more deep locks in succession to climb the cliff.

Three days after climbing the inclined plane, we're tied up in the Port de Plaisance marina in the big city of Nancy. Our barge partners have gone

VERTROUWEN up the Inclined Plane, Arzviller

home and other friends, Jim and Nancy, a couple from South Carolina, are on board for a week. Jim is 6'3" and, except for the cockpit, there's nowhere on VERTROUWEN he can stand up without stooping. Yesterday we toured Stanislas Square and the wonderful art nouveau architecture of Nancy and ate dinner at the classic Excelsior Brasserie.

Early this morning I answered a knock on the side of VERTROUWEN and met Rupert, the young British owner of the nearby barge, ALBATROSS. Rupert wants to trade positions in the marina with VERTROUWEN so a crane can set his new diesel engine into ALBATROSS' engine compartment. Rupert and his girlfriend arrived in Nancy a month ago on their way to Paris, his first cruise as owner of the ALBATROSS. Rupert says he knows nothing of engines or boat maintenance, so he hired an auto garage to send a mechanic over to change the oil in ALBATROSS' diesel engine. Rupert paid the mechanic upon completion of the job and, next day cranked up to leave for Paris. He was only a few hundred yards out of the marina when the engine "seized up" and ALBATROSS coasted to a stop. He was towed back in and he called the auto garage, who sent another mechanic to look at the engine. This mechanic told Rupert that the first mechanic had removed the old oil filter element, put in new oil, but must have forgotten to install a new oil filter element. When the engine was started, all the oil was pumped into the bilge, and the engine didn't run very long before the metal parts either melted or were fused together. Rupert raised hell with the auto garage owner and demanded a new engine, but the owner told him he had no responsibility for mistakes made by his mechanics. A lawsuit was in progress, but Rupert's lawyer told him it would take at least a year for the trial to take place, and he probably wouldn't win anyway. In desperation Rupert ordered a new engine from England and it's to arrive today. I offer my sympathy for his problem and agree to exchange places with him.

It's Sunday and we're underway from Nancy to Toul. Just as we round a bend outside Nancy, we're facing a closely packed line of fishermen along the right bank of the canal, as far as my eye can see. There must be two hundred of them, all sitting on their combination seats and tackle boxes, their net creels hanging in the water and their great long fiberglass poles extended three fourths of the way across the canal. It must be a tournament. There's no way we can get by without them moving their poles. There's nothing we can do but run this gauntlet of fishermen, scowling at our American ensign. Mary and Nancy sit on the bow, smiling and waving, trying to be friendly. Just before we run over the first fisherman's cork, he slides his pole back a few feet, and this procedure is repeated all down the line. When we're less than halfway along, a man with a bugle steps out and blows a long loud note, which must signal the end of the tournament, because all of the fishermen begin to put away their gear, smile, laugh, hold up their wine glasses and shout, "Tres beau bateau, Americain." The French are certainly serious about their fishing, although I haven't seen many fish caught all summer, and I would hesitate to eat any fish that lives in these polluted canals, where no boats have holding tanks.

At Toul, VERTROUWEN is tied up at a Port de Plaisance which has full facilities, even a boules court beside the quay. I've watched the French play their most popular sport, but never tried the game myself. The male half of the crews of two British sailboats, tied up behind us, approach my friend Jim, and ask him if we know the game and would we like to play. He lies and says we've not only played but are pretty good at it. The court is a packed gravel surface about the size of a shuffleboard court. The object is to roll steel balls, about the size of baseballs but heavier, as close as possible to a wooden marble. Each person on a two man team gets a chance to roll two steel boules, and the team that ends up closest to the wooden marble gets points. I've watched the French pros do backhanded rolls, time after time, to within centimeters of their target, and I've seen the next pro scatter the first pro's boule with a perfect bomb. Jim and I find our game lacking in the precision and finesse of the pros, but we still manage a tie with the Brits, who aren't so hot either. We decide to buy a set of boules to keep on board.

Jim and Mac take on the Englishmen in boules, Toul, 1995

It's September now and we've completed the summer's return voyage down the Canal de l'Est and River Saone to St. Symphorien, where we're again tied up at Bourgogne Marine. We've fallen in love with this life on the canals of beautiful France. Traveling the canals wasn't difficult, and magnificent scenery and interesting towns make the experience well worth the effort. During our first season on VERTROUWEN we traveled 1100 kilometers and passed through 331 locks. As we store the varnished trim boards below and cover VERTROUWEN with tarps for the winter, we're already planning an itinerary for next year.

Chapter 11

Vertrouwen to the South of France

We're back aboard VERTROUWEN on May 10, 1996, preparing to put her in the dry-dock at St Jean de Losne, to paint the bottom. The dry-dock is opened only once a week, to let boats in and out. This dry-dock is located near the top of the first lock above the River Saone, along the Canal Bourgogne. When water from the Canal Bourgogne is let in and allowed to flood the basin, completed boats motor out and other boats motor in. The entrance is then blocked off and water is allowed to pour out the back of the dry-dock and into the river Saone, below. The boats in the dry-dock are now supported on blocks, previously placed under their hulls by a diver.

VERTROUWEN in Philippe's drydock, St. Jean de Losne

Before VERTROUWEN'S bottom is painted, we're having a *sondage*, a hull thickness test, done to make sure there aren't any thin spots which may need welded plates. Some boat insurance companies require a sondage every few years. A lady and her assistant mark off a chalk grid on VERTROUWEN'S old bottom, grind the old paint off each spot to be tested and use an ultrasonic tester to check the thickness of each spot. When she presents the test report, we're distressed to find out there are a series of readings along the starboard turn of the bilge, which are a little less than the minimum safe thickness of 4 millimeters. That means we need to have some 5 millimeter plates welded over the top of the old plates, a common but expensive fix. VERTROUWEN'S 90-year-old riveted iron hull has been patched so many times that all of the rivets have been covered up with welded steel plate. The worst news comes when Philippe, the dry-dock owner, tells us he doesn't have time to do the welding now. He suggests we make our planned cruise and come back to him in the fall. We wait out the rest of the week in the dry-dock, repainting the topsides and having two coats of pungent coal tar paint rolled over the bottom. Living in the drydock is no picnic. The boatyard is dirty and noisy, and we periodically empty honeybuckets rather than use the boatyard's Eastern Toilet.

We get to know the owners of another barge in the dry-dock, who are here to have emergency repairs made to the bottom of their boat. They had received a call in England, saying that their boat, which is listed for sale, was taking on water. Afraid it would sink, they hurried over and put the boat in dry-dock just in time to discover holes and thin places scattered over the entire bottom. The value of their boat has suddenly dropped seventy five per cent. There's nothing for them to do but try to sell it to someone who can afford a whole new bottom.

Our plan this year is to travel up the Canal Bourgogne and Yonne River, and be back at the dry-dock in St. Jean de Losne by mid-September. We're underway headed toward Dijon. The canal maintenance people are mowing grass alongside the canal, and it's blowing into the canal, several times clogging the pipe that circulates cooling water to VERTROUWEN'S engine. It's a pain to stop the boat, clear out the cockpit, remove the teak grates, open the steel hatches, disconnect and clean out the hoses and put the whole thing back together. Some day, I'm going to come up with a better system.

Approaching the city of Dijon, we have to pass through a lock right at the end of the main runway of an airport. Today, Mirage fighter jets are practicing touch-downs and kicking in their afterburners just as they pass over us. I can see why the lock is automated, because no eclusier could stand that much noise on a regular basis. We tie up in Dijon at a crowded marina with a most unpleasant dockmaster, who mistakenly thinks he recognizes VERTROUWEN as a barge that left the marina last year without paying the bill. We're glad to get away next morning into the beautiful, more rural countryside. Tractors are baling and stacking hay and towing loaded carts toward a barn.

VERTROUWEN and Chateauneuf, Bourgogne Canal, 1996

We reach Vandenesse, near the summit of Canal Bourgogne, the highest canal elevation in France. We rendezvous with Peter and Mary, the British owners of COLIBRI, a barge they operate for charter. We had first met them when we were cruising on ROCINANTE. They sleep in the aft cabin with their cat and two parrots, renting out the two forward staterooms for week-long cruises on the canal. They bought COLIBRI as an old commercial peniche and spent

3 years fixing it up themselves. From this perfect mooring along the canal bank in the shade of sycamores, we can look up a steep grassy hill to the walled town and citadel at Chateauneuf. We stay several days, exploring the rolling green countryside around Vandenesse and Chateauneuf, before negotiating the last locks to the summit. These are the only locks on the canal, where we operate all gates and sluices by hand, with no help from an eclusier.

At the summit, the canal enters a 2-mile long tunnel carved through solid rock. When the stoplight at the entrance to the one way tunnel turns green, we proceed slowly into darkness. We position a floodlight to bounce light off the tunnel roof. The slow beat of the engine echoes in the tunnel, and there's a hollow sound from wavelets sloshing against the walls. Drops of water from overhead thump VERTROUWEN'S canvas cockpit. After awhile, we see a pinpoint of light ahead, slowly increasing in size, as the circle of light behind us fades away. Within a half hour we're out of the darkness of the tunnel, trying to adjust our eyes to blinding sunlight.

Entering the 2-mile tunnel of the Bourgogne Canal

We're descending from the summit now. We cruise along placidly, and typical days pass with unnautical entries in VERTROUWEN'S log :

"Friday, July 5, 1996—Visited medieval village of St. Thibault and the part of the 14th century basilica that remains. All but the choir and entrance to the north transept collapsed in the 17th century. The little stone town is dying slowly, with no shops except a boulangerie. I can see fragments of the collapsed church built into other structures. The church entrance and interior have beautiful stone and wood carvings. Each of two big carvings, deep bas relief, contain dozens of painted figures. Each group of figures is carved from a single block of wood, 12 feet long, 2 feet wide and 8 inches thick.

Underway 1100. After two miles we enter a narrow section in a deep cut with high stone walls and a forest on top. Just as we come out of the cut a bolt of lightning crashes in the forest behind us and the bottom drops out of the sky. We approach a lock and the drenched eclusier puts us through. Tie up at Pont Royal Port de Plaisance at 1215 (4 km, 1 lock). Galley stove ceased to work. Took entire stove apart, tried everything, even considered a trip to Dijon to buy a new one. Last resort was to move stove out from bulkhead, discovered it wasn't anchored in place at all; in fact, it had slid back against the wall, kinking a soft rubber gas hose and cutting off the supply, which explains why we had more and more trouble with the oven thermostat and the burners. Now, it works perfectly. It's in almost rebuilt condition, and I recovered my favorite corkscrew, which had fallen behind the stove (see May 14).

Saturday—Underway 0945. Stopped before Lock 16 at 1130. Underway 1330. Tied up to bollards in Marigny Cahouet at 1715. (12 km, 13 locks).One eclusier covered all the locks by bicycle. Mary did last five or so on foot. She is tired.

Sunday—Rainy day. Rode bike to Semur-en-Auxois and back, 15 mi. Grilled filet mignon for dinner.

Monday—In a.m., toured the town and adjacent chateau, which receives the VERTROUWEN Chateau of the Month award. Moat all of the way around, with no floating plastic bags or leaves in the water; four restored overhanging crappers embedded in a stone turret; nice glazed roof tiles; stone walls well pointed; playground equipment in courtyard; long avenue of old trees. In pm. I walked to Ste. Columbe and to Arnay Vitteaux and back, 10 miles of hills, a beautiful and isolated route. The wheat harvest looks promising. Barometer up.

Tuesday—Sunny day. Underway 0930. Tie up to bollards in Pouillenay at 1645. (6 km, 19 locks). This village has more and larger buildings than Marigny, but is practically a dead town. A closed restaurant for sale, food store closed, many empty buildings. It must be true that the demise of the small farmer, the proliferation of the supermarkets, and the flight of the young people to the cities is killing towns that don't have some particular attraction for tourism. Pouillenay is the closest town to a stone quarry that is still in operation, but probably run on a much smaller scale than previously, when stone was a material people could afford to build with.

Wednesday—Rain again. We walked up to Flavigny and back, 8 mi. Flavigny is a medieval town, which is surviving and undergoing continuing restoration as a second home for a colony of French, Swiss, and others. Beautiful limestone buildings from all periods, starting with the 9th century. We visited an anis bonbon factory, housed in a former abbey. Ate lunch at The Grange, a sort of plat du jour cafeteria, run by local ladies who do all of the cooking, serve it on trays and collect money. We sat on benches at long tables; as a result, meeting Anita, an attractive Swiss lady with henna dyed hair and oval shaped eyeglasses. She lives in Bern with Husband #1, but may be spending a lot more time in the future in Italy with Husband #2. She and Husband #1 own a beautifully restored 18th century house in Flavigny, where she comes to read and consider her future. We took tea at her house and she showed us through the rooms, with stone and ancient tile floors, fireplaces, a spiral stone and wood stair, paneled doors with original hardware, an arched stone niche containing a lavatory, built-in armoires and desks, and a magnificent attic with huge old exposed wood trusses, supporting the tile roof. The rooms were sparsely furnished, but in good taste. Anita, probably about fifty, rides her motor scooter from the train station in Montbard when she makes the trip from Bern.

Thursday—Thick fog. Underway 0900. Fog burned off. Nice day, barometer 996 and steady. Tied up to bank at Venarey les Laumes at 1215. (3 km, 10 locks). For all practical purposes this is the end of the closely spaced lock series, forty locks in 15 kilometers. All the locks were operated by the same traveling eclusier, a pleasant college student from Lorient. He and Mary did all of the work with the gates and sluices, while I sat in the cockpit beside the tiller, reading *Moby Dick*.

Whenever locks are close together Mary walks or rides a bike between locks, sometimes carrying the handheld VHF radio and calling back to let me know when the lock gates are ready to open or if there's a big peniche or hotel boat in the lock, heading our way. Her French is good enough to pass the time of day with the eclusier, much better than mine. I'm learning French, little by little, as necessary to shop or find out what I need to know. I wish I was fluent and could understand the sometimes rapid responses to my simple questions. One day, a passing French cyclist asked me a question I couldn't understand, and I replied, "*Je ne sais pas*"—I do not know. He replied in good English, "Do you mean you do not know the answer to my question? Or do you mean you do not speak French?" He was a friendly fellow, but gave me a lecture that Americans should try harder to learn foreign languages. I agree, but my old brain forgets in winter the French I learn in summer.

One midsummer evening near Montbard, we moor VERTROUWEN behind FLEUR DE LYS, one of the massive hotel barges operating along the Bourgogne Canal. We hear the unmistakable sound of American laughter reverberating from the barge and catch a glimpse of four formally dressed couples lounging on the top deck, downing drinks and telling jokes, waiting for one of their $3000 a week gourmet dinners being prepared below. As we're sipping our usual $1.75 bottle of Cote du Rhone, an unmistakable southern female voice drawls, "Are you'all really from Charleston?" A couple from the barge, carrying their long stemmed glasses of white wine, approach VERTROUWEN'S side yard, oohin and ahin about how lucky we are and how they can hardly believe we're traveling up and down the canals on our own little ole boat, so far from South Carolina. They introduce themselves as Desiré and Trent, from Tupelo, Mississippi. Just then it starts to rain and Desiré, hitching up her long black skirt, hurries back to the gangplank of the FLEUR DE LYS, waving "Bye" and saying, "Now whenever y'all are in Tupelo, you be sure to come see us, y' heah."

The summer passes too quickly and we're back in St. Jean de Losne in early September. Philippe, the dry-dock owner, says he's still too busy to weld VERTROUWEN'S bottom, and wants to put us off until next spring. To Philippe's dismay, we get a better bid from a competing boatyard and make arrangements to have the work done there next April. We return VERTROUWEN to Bourgogne Marine for the winter.

It's May, 1997, and I'm living alone on VERTROUWEN, perched high and dry above the river bank, on a marine railway at CBV Shipyard. Although M. Levec, the manager, initially expressed concerns about the condition of VERTROUWEN'S bottom, his men will begin to weld today. In accordance with his instructions, I've removed the wood bottoms from the starboard cabinets, and the floors of the hanging locker and starboard bed. Apparently, there's a fire hazard from this welding operation. M. Levec says I'm to remain inside the boat with a water bucket while the welding goes on. The blue clad workmen, after long coffee breaks and discussions pertaining to a baby swan trying to find its mother, muscle the first of the bent steel plates into place and tack weld it to VERTROUWEN'S existing bottom. I can hear the popping of welding rods and smell the melting grease that coats the inside of the bilge. A little column of acrid smoke begins to rise from the bilge. I squirt the hot spot with water from a Windex bottle and listen to it sizzle. This process goes on all day, until the plates have been jacked into their final position. Then, three welding machines start continuous welds around the edges of the new plates. It's really getting hot in here. I'm running back and forth with my squirt bottle, thinking things may be getting out of hand. I'm practicing my French for, "Stop, we're on fire." Finally, it's over and the workmen go home. The next day M. Levec inspects the work and tells me there should be no more trouble. His office prepares a tremendous bill, which takes many trips to the ATM machine to pay. The railway lowers VERTROUWEN back into the water and I motor back to Bourgogne Marine.

Mary, her brother Ned, and her father, now 93, arrive on June 1. Ned and Mr. Shower plan to spend a week on VERTROUWEN. Before we leave Bourgogne Marine, I introduce Ned to THE BREAD LADY. Every morning about 0830, a white truck speeds down the road past the moored boats, tooting its horn. The truck turns around at the end of the road and begins a slow return. Almost all of the men, seldom any women, gather on the road beside their boats, awaiting THE BREAD LADY. She stops her truck and opens the back window from the inside. There she is, blonde ponytail, red lipstick, smelling of perfume, smiling. Men forget what they've come to order. She flirts in lilting French, leaning down to make change, just a bit of cleavage and the slight touch of her palm. Her white poodle, with a red ribbon, sits beside her. She closes the window and drives away. She's made the day for many a man.

Ned and Mr. Shower, River Saone, 1997

Ned is also interested in the old abandoned dry-dock at the end of our marina basin, which is used to cut derelict commercial peniches into scrap. There are two old hulks in there now. Because there are too many commercial barges competing for an ever shrinking freight market, the French Government offers owners of old peniches cash payments in return for allowing their barges to be scrapped. They're towed into places like this, stripped, burned, cut up into pieces and hauled away. I've explored several of them and found usable pieces of mahogany and brass. It's sad that they have to end this way.

While Mr. Shower and Ned are aboard, we'll cruise from St. Symphorien to Chalon-sur-Saone, with a stop on the way in the charming little town of Seurre. We take some side trips in the rental car, wheeling Mr. Shower to the sights and restaurants in a fold-up wheelchair, although he can still walk short distances. As Mary drives the car from Seurre to Chalon, the rest of us motor VERTROUWEN down the wide river. We're entering the only lock we'll go through today. Mr. Shower and I are in the cockpit and Ned's on the foredeck to handle the lines. We slowly approach a wall of the wide lock and Ned loops a line over a bollard and back to a bit on deck. He knows he'll have to slack off on the line, as the water level drops. A commercial peniche enters the lock, behind us. The gates close. Ned is looking back, not paying attention, when the water level begins to drop. The end of the rope catches around VERTROUWEN'S steel bit and cinches tight before Ned can prize it off. Now the rope is supporting the whole weight of VERTROUWEN'S bow, and we're beginning to tilt up at an angle, as the water drops further. I run below, grab a butcher knife and head toward the bow, when there's a loud pop and our bow falls back into the water. Thank God for rotten ropes. There's no harm done, except to the rope and Ned's pride. As a former Navy sailor on aircraft carriers, ice breakers and ammunition ships, he's highly embarrassed.

After Ned and Mr. Shower leave Chalon in a rental car, Mary and I continue down the Saone, headed toward this year's destination, the Midi Canal, which connects the Mediterranean Sea to the Atlantic Ocean. We've made this trip down the Saone and Rhone before on ROCINANTE. After passing Tournus we make a detour up the River Seille, a tributary of the Saone, which we've not seen before. It's a beautiful little river with just a few locks, and we tie up at a quay in the town of Louhans, at the upper end of the river.

Yesterday, Sunday, Louhans was a sleepy little town, but this morning it's teeming with people, headed for the weekly market. Not many tourists here, just the great weather-beaten faces of local folks from the countryside, getting off buses with shopping baskets or poucettes or parking their cars and trucks to walk into the center of town. It's the liveliest and most extensive market we've seen in France, with blocks and blocks of outdoor stalls, selling everything—all types of food, clothing, furniture, farm machinery, kitchen utensils, live chickens, dead chickens and chickens cooking on a spit. At the center of town, in the blocks surrounding the church, stalls are set up under the sidewalk arcades of old three story stone buildings. Crowds fill the streets and a hurdy gurdy man grinds out traditional tunes, as a poodle sleeps on top of his machine.

The market closes down soon after noon and we move VERTROUWEN back down the river, to a more peaceful spot along a grassy bank. It's so quiet here I can hear church bells in six distant towns striking the hour, each at a slightly different time. The songs of birds fill the air, but I recognize only the cuckoos, doves and crows. This is a perfect place to spend a week of solitude. We ride our bikes along country roads and through tiny villages, stopping for a beer at the Daffy Duck Cafe.

At Lyon, where the Saone meets the Rhone, we're tied up in front of HOSANNA, a big fully rigged sailing tjalk, belonging to Bill and Laurel Cooper, a British couple who've written many sailing and travel books, including Sell Up and Sail, which I read many years ago before our first voyage on ROCINANTE. They've completed another book about traveling down the

Danube River, their worst trip yet according to them. Now he's considering trying to sail HOSANNA across the Atlantic, a most unlikely feat, I would think, in such an old flat bottomed boat.

Repas on the quiet River Seille

Running with the current, we pass quickly down the Rhone. We stop for a few days below the Palace of the Popes in the wonderful walled city of Avignon before turning into the Petite Rhone. We enter a marshy delta known as the Camargue, where young fighting bulls grow up before entering the ring. We stop just before the medieval walled city of Aigues Mortes, once a major port on the Mediterranean Sea, where the fifth Crusade was launched. Years later, the Med silted in and the shoreline shifted, leaving Aigues Mortes stranded and land locked. Only a 2-mile canal now connects Aigues Mortes to the sea.

A large American barge that we've seen several times before, the PURSUIT DE BONHEUR, approaches from behind and stops beside us. Her owner, actor Darren McGavin, tells us he ran into a bridge under construction outside of Avignon. His port side is bent, three windows broken and several stanchions destroyed. He's 76-years-old, crippled and practically blind as a bat, but he's making his lifelong dream of sailing his own boat to the south of France come true. He's still not deterred and wants to know who he can call on his cellphone to come fix his boat. His only crew, a young Brit who was hired as chef but who has had to do everything from maintaining the engine to steering the boat and handling the lines, is more concerned about PURSUIT DE BONHEUR than Darren is. PURSUIT DE BONHEUR ties up to the bank a little way in front of us.

Descending in a deep lock with too short a line

A few days later, after helping Darren Magavan find a repair yard in Grau du Roi, we continue paralleling the Mediterranean coast toward Sete. Only a narrow strip of sand and shallow salt water lakes, called Etangs, separate us from the Mediterranean Sea. We tie up to a concrete wall near the ancient Maguelonne Abbaye, which sits on a high sand dune, overlooking the sea. Between us and the abbaye is a wide etang, full of pink flamingoes standing in the shallow water.

Another familiar barge is approaching, the GOLDEN THISTLE. She's a beautifully restored tjalk, her hull paint and brightwork perfect. The mate stands on the foredeck in a bikini, ready to throw a line. The bald elderly captain sits by the tiller with a long stemmed glass of white wine, shouting instructions, "Jump off," he orders in an upper class English accent. She ignores him and waits for someone on shore to show an interest in catching a line. An offshore wind is pushing GOLDEN THISTLE toward the wrong bank. The captain stands, upsetting his wine glass, which tumbles down the companionway stair, breaking into pieces. "Jean, you'll have some tidying up to do. If you can't seem to get us tied up, then bring me another glass of wine, please." She throws a bowline to someone on shore and together, they finally haul GOLDEN THISTLE to moor against the wall.

We met Douglas and Jean earlier, in Avignon. They're both London barristers. He's 80 while she's at least 25 years younger. They had looked for a long time for a classic tjalk to have restored and when she found one, she left a note in his "wig box," saying she was on her way to finalize the deal to buy it. They've spared no expense in the restoration, using part of a salvaged ballroom floor from an English manor house as the cabin sole, building in formal mahogany furniture and installing a beveled glass shower door etched with a thistle. We had previously accepted an invitation for wine aboard GOLDEN THISTLE and been offered our choice of red, white or rose from built-in vats with spigots.

The GOLDEN THISTLE

Today is like summer at Pawleys Island, hot sun with a slight sea breeze, freshening in the late morning. We ride our bikes to the beach, the Grande Bleu, and sit on a towel, sunbathing and listening to seagulls and small birds in the bushes. The water temperature is almost warm enough to swim. Before lunch we walk our bikes across a movable pontoon bridge to the other side of the canal and ride into the town of Villeneuve to provision. The afternoon is too hot to do much except lie still in VERTROUWEN'S cockpit. Across from us is a fish camp, where French fishermen return from the etangs in wooden runabouts with their nets and buckets of little yellow fish. They sit in front of a rough shack, drinking pastis and waiting for a daily visit from the tank truck, which takes their catch away to market.

After a week on the beach at Maglione we get underway, southwestward through the port city of Sete, too full of highrises and tourists to be of much interest. We're ready to cross the Etang de Thau, the largest of the shallow lakes, 20 miles long and 5 miles wide. It can be rough in windy weather but today it's calm. We use a hand bearing compass to steer toward the lighthouse at the other end. To starboard are vast rows of pipe racks sticking up out of the water, supporting strings that grow thousands of delicious oysters. Before reaching the end of Etang de Thau we turn to starboard and enter the harbor of the fishing village of Marseillan. There are several ocean going sailboats moored here. They can cross the etang and enter the Med through the entrance at Sete.

Across from the quay where VERTROUWEN is tied up is the Hotel le Chateau du Port, a handsome four story stone building. We celebrate Mary's birthday at the hotel restaurant with a lunch of moules marinière, salade verte and a very nice local white wine. The classic 19th century interior of the hotel has a spiral marble staircase in the lobby and many colorful sailboat pennants hanging from fine mahogany woodwork in the bar.

Climbing the seven ecleuses of Beziers

A few days later, after a tour of the Noilly Prat vermouth factory, we leave Marseillan, exit the Etang de Thau and head toward VERTROUWEN'S winter destination, Port la Robine, a marina not far from Narbonne. After a stop in the city of Bezier. we prepare to climb a series of locks to the Canal du Midi, one of the oldest canals in France. From VERTROUWEN'S log:

"Thursday, July 24—Underway 0930. Stopped at bottom of seven ecluses at 0945, to wait. Started up the seven interconnected locks at 1045. Water roars down from one lock to the next as the gates ahead are opened, exciting but not dangerous. Tied up to bank at Colombiers at 1230 (8 km, 8 locks). Nice little town. Has eclectic church with artifacts dating back to the Romans and Visigoths. The canal is a tunnel, lined on both sides with big sycamore trees, whose ancient roots crawl down the banks and into the water. Visited tourist office in abandoned wine aging warehouse, with great arched wooden roof and huge wooden barrels.

Friday—Hiked to Oppidum d'Enserune, occupied since the 6th century BC. Excavations began in the 1920's. Wonderful museum of artifacts, and a view of distant mountains and Mediterranean Sea. Below is Montady Etang, wheel shaped, with spoke ditches drained by tunnel, built in 1200 AD. Reve de France hireboat base is near VERTROUWEN. All rented boats had to be returned today, a madhouse of bumpboats. Overlooking marina is a plate glass window of second floor coiffure, where two ladies are being prepped. There are more than thirty boats in the marina. 28 teenagers just arrived to board four hireboats for an excursion to Carcassonne, replacing the same number, who left earlier. Fortunately, the rattle of windblown sycamore leaves drowns out the kids' voices and rock and roll music.

Saturday—Underway 0915, before hireboat exodus. Tie up to wall in Poilhes in front of another tjalk at 1030 (6 km, 0 locks, 1 tunnel). Judy, previous owner of PURSUIT DE BONHEUR, visited to enquire about Darren McGavin's progress. Through a porthole I see two pairs of

Parking-metered water, Midi Canal

bright red toenails protruding from silver sandals. One trips over our docking line and Mary gives an attractive Norwegian lady a wet kleenex to wash her scraped knee. They're very friendly, speaking English, no French. Steve and Kitty, of the VROUWE JEANNETTE behind us, visited. They've been moored here since last October. View from here, over the valley to the distant mountains, is superb. Fed 10 franc coins into American parking meter at quayside faucet to pay for metered water.

Sunday—Lunch in a family restaurant. Outside tables are taken, so we are set up in the main room, inside, which is the bar, and has a long table where the family eats. The decor is mounted bull's heads and bullfight photos and posters. A big loaf of country bread is put on top of our bare wood table, followed by a plate of ham, saucisson and pate and butter, and a plate of tomatoes and onions, with a pichet of red wine, all served by various members of three generations of the family. Later, cassoulet of white beans, sausage, spare ribs, and a jar of pickles on the side. The proprietor stands at the bar, tossing down five or six pastis, in conversation with a friend. Dessert is a fudge sickle and coffee. Not 3-star, but interesting. Afterwards, sat on a bench in the shade with locals, watching hireboats bumbling by.

We arrive at our destination, Port la Robine marina, and are met by Ted, the Australian manager who looks like a character out of a Joseph Conrad novel, bushy gray beard, gold tooth, earring, fading tattoos, weatherbeaten face, rheumy eyes and a slight tremble of the hands. He helps us tie up under a pine tree and, in spite of the heat we varnish, clean and touch up VERTROUWEN, preparing to leave her with our partners. When our partners arrive, we catch a ride to the train station in Narbonne, take the TGV to Paris, transfer to a train to Brittany, catch a local train and a bus to Roscoff, just in time for the midnight ferry to Port Cobh, Ireland. After the overnight ferry trip, accompanied by 2000 other passengers and 600 cars, we're met by Adrian, the friend we first got to know, sailing ROCINANTE along the Atlantic coast of Spain.

Since then, Adrian has bought DOM PERIGNON, a Salar 40 sloop, which he's graciously invited us to borrow for 2 weeks. She's a comfortable motor sailer, which Adrian shows us how to operate, as we sail from Kinsale to Bantry. Adrian seems to have no concerns about us taking his boat alone along the southwest coast of Ireland. I express some concern that most of his charts are as old as VERTROUWEN, but he declares that the rocks haven't moved. We dinghy him ashore and we're off from Bantry, to cruise to many of the same places we visited in ROCINANTE in 1992.

Ireland's coast from DOM PERIGNON

Mary writes in her journal, "The southwestern coast of Ireland is probably the most beautiful coastline I've ever seen. Each headland, each bay, each island, has its own character. It's never boring, always another surprise awaiting you. The more gentle land of West Cork gradually gives way to the higher and more rugged profile of the Beara Peninsula between Bantry Bay and the Kenmare River. Between large areas of gorse and heather is green velvet pastureland, turned into a patchwork quilt by an irregular gridwork of stone fences. The edge of the quilt ends abruptly, as if ground off by giants' teeth. What's left are large vertical slabs of rock, sculpted during the Ice Age, protecting the greenness of Ireland from the pounding of the Atlantic Ocean."

We particularly enjoy revisiting Castletownbere, even though rainy weather forces us to spend too much time in Mary McCarthy's Grocery and Bar. Fishing boats and sailboats slip in and out of this harbor at all times of the day and night. Last night, after midnight I heard the rattle of an anchor chain near us. This morning, I see a big green ketch, her home port listed as Basel, Switzerland, named TECTOJA. She has a little wheelhouse, far aft under the mizzen boom. She's a salty old wooden boat, about 55-feet long, gaff rigged, with tanbark sails, ratlines and lots of baggy wrinkle. It's the kind of boat I'd like to own and sail, but not have to maintain. She looks like she needs a lot of work.

We return to Kinsale just in time to miss some really nasty weather. Adrian and his family are very gracious to us. After touring Cork and Cobh, the port where so many Irish embarked to emigrate to America, and the last port for the TITANIC and the LUSITANIA, we fly to Plymouth. We visit with other sailing friends in Cornwall, before returning to Paris to catch a flight back to South Carolina.

Chapter 12

The Next Generation

We've given up the idea of building a French farmhouse. In the fall of 1997 we sell our house in Mt. Pleasant and buy back and move into our original condominium at Belle Isle, where we first started cruising in 1975. I consider the condo as a temporary base and a place to store our furniture and mementos. I'd really rather live on a boat, maybe a trawler, and make a circumnavigation of the eastern half of the United States and go to the Bahamas and back any time we want to. I begin to look in boating magazines at ads for used trawlers.

Mary is busy preparing for a one woman show of her photographs of the French canals, which she has been invited to give at Charleston's City Gallery. She's also helping with our first grandchild, Alexandra, who was born to Leigh and Jamie in November.

One day I drive to Beaufort to look at an advertised trawler, which turns out to be a big tub with a useless mast. While walking the docks I see a big green trawler that catches my eye. From the outside she looks a lot like a

The trawler MARY M

commercial fishing boat. When the owner steps off the boat, I ask him about her and he tells me she's for sale. He built her of steel and fitted her out on Lake Michigan 4 years ago. Now, he and his wife are living aboard and headed down the Intracoastal Waterway. I like her looks, her 50-foot green hull with a forward wheelhouse with windows that slant in. She looks something like the boat in the movie, *The Perfect Storm.* The owner shows me the interior, simple but well trimmed out in mahogany, a handsome wheelhouse with all of the electronics I could ever want, a big main salon, modern galley, plenty of sleeping space below and a huge engine room, where I can actually walk, not crawl, around the two John Deere diesels and the diesel generator. The aft stateroom and aft head aren't finished yet. I can see real possibilities for Mary and me to live on her part of the year, cruising the ICW, Great Lakes and Bahamas. We might even give up our interest in VERTROUWEN to spend more time on her.

I return to Belle Isle, so enthusiastic that Mary agrees to look at the trawler the next weekend. We drive to Savannah, take another look and Mary likes it too. Her biggest concern is whether the two of us can handle a 50-foot boat but, with twin engines we shouldn't have any trouble. We decide to think it over.

In December, Robert asks me to help him and the owner of a 48-foot Hinckley ketch deliver it from Charleston to Man-O-War Cay. I jump at the chance to get another look at the island and Pirates Den. We get underway with a favorable wind and make a fast and easy passage, less than 3 days. The owner, a doctor from Myrtle Beach, S.C., becomes so enthralled by his first visit to Man-O-War that he's talking about moving there and becoming a resident physician for the Abacos. On our way back from Florida in a rental car Robert and I stop in Jacksonville to take another look at the green trawler, which is still on its way down the ICW. Robert thinks it would make a great fishing boat. After we get home, Mary and I again discuss buying the trawler and decide to make an offer. After some negotiation with the owner about finishing the aft stateroom, we agree on a price, a survey is done and we're to take possession in July, 1998.

On May 1, 1998 we're back aboard VERTROUWEN, getting her ready to continue west, along the Canal du Midi, toward Bordeaux. We don't plan to go very far because we have to be back in South Carolina before July. After our first day of travel we're tied up in Homps, hoping to see BERENDINA, a charter barge bought last year by sailing friends of ours from the U.S. Virgin Islands. Neil and Katherine drive up just as we're getting ready to leave, and we spend the day aboard BERENDINA, talking about old times. Neil, my age, owned and operated a sailing day charter business in St. Thomas for 30 years. He had a wooden character schooner built in Nevis, the ALEXANDER HAMILTON, which he was chartering in Red Hook when I met him. Two years ago a hurricane sank the ALEXANDER HAMILTON, with Neil and Katherine aboard. They had to swim to another boat. A few months after the storm, they had telephoned us and talked about buying a barge and chartering in France. They used the insurance money from ALEXANDER HAMILTON to buy BERENDINA. She's a beautiful barge, but Neil says he's having trouble handling her under the low arched brick bridges of the Midi. He rounded off the corners of the top of his wheelhouse but tells me as we're leaving, "I hope I haven't taken on more than I can chew."

Bridge on the Canal du Midi

The locks of the Midi, many built in the 1600's, are oval shaped rather than rectangular, making it more difficult to tie up without banging the

Oval shaped stone walls of the Midi Canal locks

bow or stern of VERTROUWEN into the stone lock walls. Even though it's early in the season there's quite a lot of traffic—sailboats and pleasure powerboats using this shortcut to avoid having to sail all of the way around Spain. We watch a big Dutch cruiser with a high wheelhouse trying to get under one of the old arched bridges. The boat's deck is loaded with barrels of water to sink her down to the bottom, and she's plowing through the mud. Right now, there's plenty of water in the canal but sometimes, during the dry season of mid summer, when the farmers pump their irrigation water out of the canal, the Midi becomes too shallow for most boats. No commercial peniches use the Midi.

We continue west and up past Carcassonne and Castlenaudry to the summit of the canal, where there is a beautiful forest and an obelisk honoring the Midi's builder, Pierre Paul Riquet. He started building the canal in 1667 during the reign of Louis XIV, but used up all of his own money and died before it was completed in 1681. His designs for lock gates and water retention ponds are the basis for the present French canal system.

We stop in Toulouse, the biggest city in this part of France, to meet friends who will spend a week aboard VERTROUWEN. They drive up in a rental car, which we'll bike back to retrieve after each day's short journey. The car is useful for exploring places too far away to walk or bike to. This afternoon, after a short cruise, Joe, a nervous driver, chauffeurs us to Cahors to view an ancient bridge over the River Lot. On the way back, we pass a village where a carnival or festival is in progress. We decide to investigate, and Joe follows a big tour bus up a narrow street toward the festivities. The street becomes so congested that the bus has to stop. Joe stops the little Renault Clio a few feet behind the bus. The bus shifts into reverse, its backup lights flashing and horn beeping. The Clio is too close for the bus driver to see us. Joe panics, beating on the steering wheel, where the horn would normally be located, and yelling out of the window. He's trying to shift into reverse but it won't go into gear. We watch helplessly as the bus backs up slowly but surely, stopping only when the driver hears a crunch of metal behind him. The bus driver nonchalantly smokes a cigarette and fills out the accident report, admitting it was his fault. We return the still drivable Clio to Toulouse, where a nice rental lady replaces the car and routinely instructs Joe that the horn button is on the end of the turn signal and you must pull out on the gearshift lever to shift into reverse.

A week later we leave the Canal Midi, locking down into the Baise River. The Baise River was made into a navigable canal in the 1800's, so that armagnac, the local brandy could be transported down the river in barges to market. Now only pleasure boats travel up the river as far as the unfortunately named town of Condom. The river is narrow with steep tree-lined banks. We're cruising toward the town of Nerac, in company with a big hireboat crewed by three French couples. Hireboats can be no longer than 15 meters (48 feet), since the French government requires that all longer boats must have licensed captains. The hireboat companies have designed 48-foot boats that look like rectangular plastic boxes and will accommodate as many as 6 or 8 people, who pay as much as $6000 a week to rent the boat. We lag behind the hireboat, but, when they stop to look at a chateau on a hill, we pass them.

Medieval town of Nerac, on the Baise River

The locks on the Baise River are just long enough for two 15-meter boats to squeeze in. At the last lock they had invited us to go in behind them. Now, they're insisting on being in this lock, behind us. Our bow is really too close to the lock gate, and their bow is touching our rudder. The lock is an automatic one, activated by lifting a rod embedded in one side of the lock wall.

Mary lifts the rod, the rear gates close and water begins to lift us. The other boat's bow pushes against our stern and VERTROUWEN'S bow is pressed against the front steel gate. The gate is reinforced by protruding horizontal steel beams. As VERTROUWEN rises, her prow catches under a steel beam and I can't back up. The water continues to rise and VERTROUWEN'S bow is tilting down, being forced under the water by the beam. Mary sees what's happening and runs to the red emergency rod and lifts it, stopping the lock from filling. The pressure of the lock beam on VERTROUWEN'S tilted bow is too much and a steel plate on our prow rips and rolls back like the top of a sardine can. Our bow springs up, producing a wave in the lock, which surges back and forth, banging the boats off the gates. When everything calms down, there's really no serious damage to either boat, other than our rolled back prow. We let the water down, the French boat backs out and we go through the lock alone. Afterwards, Mary criticizes me, "Another case of you being Mr. Nice Guy." At Nerac I pound the steel back down with a sledge hammer and touch up the paint. We'll have it rewelded next time we're in a boatyard.

After two pleasant weeks of cruising along the Baise River, we return to the Midi and head toward the town of Moissac, where our partners will take over and return VERTROUWEN to Port Robine. At Moissac we catch a train to Bordeaux, then Paris, and fly home in time to take possession of the steel trawler JONATHAN, which we rename the MARY M.

It's taking awhile to get used to the MARY M, especially learning to maneuver a 50-foot boat with two engines, knowing it's not MARY M that'll be damaged by a collision, but the boat or pier she hits. She weighs 75,000 pounds and carries 1200 gallons of fuel and 400 gallons of water. She has flopper stopper stabilizers, like a commercial boat, to reduce rolling in the ocean. Robert, Jamie, another friend and I make a fishing trip to the Gulf Stream. At her cruising speed of 8 knots it takes all night for MARY M to get there. It's a calm and perfect fishing day and we catch a big king mackerel and a bigger wahoo, along with some smaller fish. Jamie cooks the king mackerel and we have a delicious leisurely dinner as we return to Belle Isle. It's a great trip.

We make a few other short cruises on MARY M, a weekend to Edisto Island and back with Mary's father on board, and a floating birthday party-oyster roast for Alexandra's second birthday, but I spend most of my time maintaining and improving the big steel trawler. Although the aft stateroom and head have now been completed, there's still a long list of desired but expensive and time-consuming improvements to be made. It seems I'm at the marina every day, puttering around, touching up a little rust or trying to figure out some electrical circuit.

Painting MARY M's bottom, Beaufort, NC

On April 15, 1999, Mary and I and Ben the cat head north on the ICW, aboard the MARY M, destination Chesapeake Bay. Near Beaufort, North Carolina, we stop at a boatyard with a big travel lift, to pull out and paint MARY M'S bottom—such a big bottom too, two and a half gallons of bottom paint per coat. Mary and I work like crazy to sand, paint and get MARY M back in the water in 2 days. Ben hates the sound and motion of MARY M and spends most of his time trying to escape. Just as we tie up outside the Sanitary Fish Market and Restaurant in Morehead City, Ben makes a spectacular dive through a porthole screen onto the pier and flees toward the kitchen, only to be once again recaptured and restricted to dry cereal and water in solitary confinement below decks. We have an easy trip up the ICW, through the Dismal Swamp and Norfolk, to Chesapeake Bay. MARY M is more economical to run than most of the faster power boats, burning only four and a half gallons an hour, but we're barely faster than the sailboats, and we have to share their frustrations at being passed by behemoth cruisers and sports fishing boats, kicking up big wakes. MARY M is easily the most comfortable boat we've ever owned. We anchor out most nights, rather than tying up at marinas that charge over a dollar a foot per night. MARY M carries a dinghy on stern davits, making it easy to go ashore. We cruise up the Potomac River to Washington DC and spend a week at the Gangplank Marina. Mary and Ben (good riddance) leave in a rental car, returning to South Carolina to pick up Mary's father to rejoin MARY M later.

I'm joined by a friend from South Carolina and we start back down the Potomac. Jim, being a former Marine, wants to exercise his right to tie up for the night at the marina at Quantico Marine Base. I'm ordered by the military dockmaster to back MARY M into a tiny awkward slip. I remove the dinghy from the davits and try, unsuccessfully to turn MARY M'S stern around a corner. A young marine springs aboard to help, and succeeds in breaking one of MARY M'S windows with a boat hook. We're finally given The General's empty slip, which is much easier to get into. Jim and I have a good week's cruise to Baltimore and back to a marina at the mouth of the Potomac, to meet Mary and her father.

We believe this may be the last cruise for Mr. Shower. He's 95 years old, almost blind and more feeble than a year ago. We're taking him back to his old home, near Annapolis. We anchor in Weems Creek, within sight of the house on a cliff where, as a boy, he left every morning to row across the creek and catch a train to Baltimore to attend high school. He thinks he can barely see his old house through binoculars. We cruise up to Baltimore, where he was born and where he graduated from Johns Hopkins University. We tie up at the Inner Harbor Marina. Mr. Shower's 90-year-old cousin visits him on MARY M. After a week, we're back at the Coan River Marina, leaving MARY M for the summer and hurricane season, while we cruise on VERTROUWEN.

Our barge partners have cruised VERTROUWEN from Port la Robine to Aigues Mortes, where Mary and I will take over, for the slow and tortuous 200 mile journey up the Rhone River against the current. We've picked August and September, the months of least rainfall and current, for the trip. Above Avignon, our little 50 horsepower engine allows us to creep at just 3 knots. We enter the massive Bollene Lock, whose sheer concrete walls rise 80 feet above us. Earlier, we had heard that last year a gate of this lock had been opened prematurely, allowing a wall of water to crush a British sailboat, drowning one of the crew. When the gate closes, no sunlight can reach the bottom of the lock, creating an almost scary dark and hollow place. We tie VERTROUWEN'S bow and stern tightly to a floating bollard, recessed in a concrete wall. The bollards are spaced too far apart to tie onto more than one. As the water rises, turbulence swirls under our hull, and the hollow squeal from bollards scraping against their metal guides echoes from the walls.

When VERTROUWEN emerges from Bollene Lock, 80 feet higher, we begin hunting for a place to spend the night. Finally, near Viviers, we tie up to the only quay available, even though there's a sign saying "Hotel Bateau." It's late in the afternoon, the quay's empty and we figure no hotel boat will be using it tonight. Just before dark, the 250-foot hotel boat, ARLENE, appears from around the bend and heads directly for us. She gives us no warning and seems unconcerned, as she latches her bow on to a big dolphin in front of us and begins to use her stern thruster to push her port side toward us. Two feet from VERTROUWEN'S hull ARLENE'S bow stops against a high dirt bank, and her crew throws a heavy line across our roof to tie on to a shore bollard. No problem. Now we're at eye level and 2 feet away from the picture window of a lower deck stateroom, where an elderly couple stand in their underwear, dressing for dinner. They smile, wave and close their drapes.

We know we're trapped until ARLENE leaves, but fortunately she gets underway before 0800. VERTROUWEN continues fighting the Rhone current until, just before the town of Tournon, there's a big bang and rattle from the overworked engine. I shut it down and try to steer to catch on to a buoy to keep from floating backwards. I'm looking at the engine and don't see any glaring cracks so, to keep from losing more ground, I crank up and VERTROUWEN limps into the marina at Tournon. A Dutchman stands on the dock, admiring VERTROUWEN, a traditional boat of his country. I ask him about a mechanic, and he just happens to have a friend who owns a local auto repair shop and who also keeps his boat in this marina. The mechanic arrives the next day, and our Dutch friend acts as interpreter for his French. The mechanic suspects a burned fuel injector. He must complete repairs to a taxi transmission first, because both of his helpers are on vacation, but he promises to complete the job within a week. A week later, he's replaced all of the injector tips, I've cleaned out the dirty fuel filters and we're on our way again.

The current gets worse the closer we get to Lyon and, as we try to pass under a last major highway bridge, water piles up a foot high against the upstream side of the bridge abutments and slooshes between them like a Colorado River rapid. It takes almost a minute for VERTROUWEN to pass between the abutments. I wonder what would happen if VERTROUWEN looses power now. An hour later we're finally upstream of the intersection of the Rhone and the Saone, and the current slacks off considerably. The Saone is a much more placid river, where swans and mallards glide along peacefully. We make good progress to Chalon-sur-Saone, where we turn off, onto the Canal du Centre. Our destination is Decize, where we turn into the Nivernais, a canal restored for the use of pleasure boats only. It's one of the prettiest canals in France, with many quaint little towns and much beautiful rural scenery.

This afternoon we're tied up to bollards along the grassy bank of a wide place in the canal, far from any big town. The only other boat here is the CHOUETTE, a pretty hotel boat wintering here. We walk toward the closest village, Mailly le Chateau. We pass close to an old millhouse and cross the Yonne River on a 15th century stone bridge with a little chapel at its center, honoring St. Nicholas, the patron saint of boat people. There's nothing of much interest in the lower town except for a bizarre sculpture in the square, topped by a stone wolf covering its head with a paw and shedding stone tears. Holding on to a wrought iron railing, we climb a steep cobbled path between two houses, toward the upper town.

At the top of the hill is a tree shaded park with a superb view of the Yonne valley. We walk to the main square of the tiny town. On one side of the square is an elegant old hotel with a couple of expensive British cars parked out front. In the center of the square is a 12th century church which is open. The dim cool inside of the church seems frozen several centuries back in time. The stone floor, columns and vaults are as they have been for over 500 years. Finely carved wood box pews are similar in style to ones in the Carolina's Low Country early churches, once polished but now weathered with age. Roman numerals and family names are carved into some of them. A few of the rough kneeling benches are covered with tattered faded upholstery. Dark velvet drapes shield high backed kneeling chairs inside paneled confessional booths. The cracked plaster walls are lined with statues of Jeanne D'Arc, the Virgin and Stations of the Cross, sharing space with plaques dedicated to the many fallen soldiers of World War I. There are probably very few parishioners now and the church serves mainly as a museum for Pre-Revolutionary Catholicism. We continue past old limestone houses with steep terra cotta tile roofs, back down the hill to VERTROUWEN. I remove the grill and charcoal from the forward locker and get ready to cook charolais filets. We're also having grilled potatoes, a tomato and lettuce salad, a bottle of Bourgogne Coulanges-la-Vineuse, espresso and chocolate noir with hazelnuts. Ah, France.

Auxerre Cathedral, on the River Yonne

We would have dawdled in the Nivernais longer, except we're in such a hurry. We have to be in Auxerre by September 25 to meet our new barge partners. Last winter we decided to try to find a third couple to share VERTROUWEN'S expenses, thinking there's enough time in a season for three couples to share. Charlie and Lani bought a third interest in VER-

TROUWEN, sight unseen, and they're to meet us in the city of Auxerre and begin to become acquainted with VERTROUWEN. We await them at Auxerre's marina, which stretches along one shore of the wide river Le Yonne, directly across from a magnificent twelfth century cathedral, whose stone tower and the flying buttresses and stained glass of the projecting apse are brightly illuminated each night. They arrive on time and we start toward Paris, where we plan to leave VERTROUWEN for the winter. They're an athletic pair, a few years younger than we are, and have little trouble learning to operate VERTROUWEN.

We're traveling down the upper Seine, only a few miles outside of Paris in the late afternoon when I see a familiar barge, PAX ABSOLUUT, a beautiful 80-foot Dutch Luxmotor barge, rafted outside a commercial peniche along the shore. The owners, whom we had known at St Symphorien, recognize VERTROUWEN and signal us to tie alongside. Although we're supposed to have a reservation at the Arsenal Marina, it's too late to get that far today, and we accept John and Ienka's invitation to remain tied to them for the night. John and Ienka live permanently on PAX ABSOLUUT, which is as spacious and luxuriously furnished as a fine home. They also own the full sized peniche, permanently tied up to the shore next to them, which they're converting into three rental apartments. They've leased the shoreline from the Town, which is supposed to provide town water to the apartment barge, but hasn't done so yet. Because one apartment is complete and occupied, John has had to buy a big watermaker for PAX ABSOLUUT, which turns Seine river water into drinking water, and is piped into the apartment.

Although we applied for a reservation at the Arsenal Marina, we're not sure we have one, so we take John's suggestion to check out another marina, across the river from PAX ABSOLUUT before we leave to enter Paris. John rides aboard VERTROUWEN and guides us into the tiny entrance to the crowded marina. We tie up to a pier and wait for the dockmaster to find out if there are any slips available. He finally arrives and says there's a small space, if we need it. We're ready to take John back to PAX ABSOLUUT so I shift VERTROUWEN into reverse, but she doesn't budge an inch. John, who has known VERTROUWEN and her previous owner for a long time, immediately suspects that the reverse gear in the transmission is stripped. He says this happened once before, years ago, before we owned her. He says I should

VERTROUWEN in Arsenal Marina, Paris, for the Millennium

take the cover off the gearbox, while he goes to find a mechanic. After he's gone and I'm working on the gearbox, Mary, who's standing on shore, asks, "Why's VERTROUWEN"S bow so high out of the water?" I get off and look. She's right, VERTROUWEN'S aground, stuck on a rock under the bow. They must have let some water out of a Seine lock, causing the river level to fall slightly.

When John returns, saying he can't find a mechanic, he sees the problem and realizes it's not the gearbox. He walks back across a bridge to PAX ABSOLUUT, and he and Ienka work their big barge into the marina, close enough to throw us a rope. PAX ABSOLUUT'S engine strains back, and VERTROUWEN pops off the rock. We continue down the Seine into Paris and tie up outside of Arsenal Marina. We're told VERTROUWEN does have a reservation, and we tie up near the place where we spent the winter of 1992 on ROCINANTE. Reluctantly, Mary and I prepare to go home, leaving Charlie and Lani to stay a few weeks longer in Paris. Flying home, we're already sorry we can't take further advantage of VERTROUWEN'S being in Paris all winter. After our partners leave, she'll lie empty there for the rest of the winter. Wouldn't it be great to be there for the Millennium. Why couldn't we return and spend Christmas and New Years in Paris?

It's snowing when our plane lands at DeGaulle in mid-December. The inside of VERTROUWEN is only a few degrees above freezing, and the little electric heater isn't warming it up very fast. Not looking too chic in multi layers of sweatshirts and foul weather gear, we spend as much time as possible in warm museums, shops and restaurants. Despite the cold and rainy weather, Parisians flock to the stores, preparing for Christmas. Streets are decorated with thousands of lights, and crowds of people are carrying Christmas trees and presents along the sidewalks and into the Metro.

On the morning after Christmas, major storms sweep across France and through Paris. High winds damage windows and chimneys of many buildings, uproot trees and blow down holiday decorations. The boats in the marina are only slightly affected, because we're so far below street level. The biggest problem for us is caused by the large amount of rainfall, making the River Seine rise more than 10 feet, flooding the marina lock and even covering the quays where we step off the floating piers to go ashore. Finally, two days before the New Year, rising water shorts out the electricity to all of the boats on our side of the marina. Now, with the temperature right at freezing and Mary suffering a bad cold, it looks like we have a choice of moving into a hotel or going home early. Just as we're making a final decision to go home early, the dockmaster in his little dinghy begins to tow the occupied barges across to the other side of the marina, where electricity is still working. He tows us across and we have heat again. We're really glad that we don't have to leave Paris before New Years Eve, because the Millennium fireworks display on the Eiffel Tower proves to be the most spectacular extravaganza of exploding color I've ever seen, worth all of the aggravations of bad weather, boat inconveniences and teeming hordes of spectators.

During the spring of 2000, Mary's father's health takes a turn for the worse. We move MARY M from Belle Isle to Charleston and live there, to be able to take better care of him. He passes away during the summer, just shy of his 97th birthday. We make some short trips on MARY M during the season but no cruise in France this year. We have a new grandson, Jack, born to Leigh and Jamie in July.

Robert's first look at ALLIANCE's bottom

Robert, still a bachelor at 36, and I drive to Pensacola, Florida in June for a family reunion. While there, Robert spots an old wooden sailboat for sale at a marina across the Alabama line, which affects him with BOAT FEVER. He thinks he must have this boat, a 45-foot yawl. I try to talk him out of it, but she does have pretty lines. The owners, a family of missionaries, live aboard and are anxious to sell their boat and move back to Seattle. Employing her most zealous salesmanship, the missionary wife relates the miracle of last night, when she had a vision that a family with our name would come to the boat today and buy it and live happily ever after. They reduce the price and, a week later, with some financial help from me, Robert buys the boat, without a marine survey.

Another 500 mile drive to Josephine, Alabama, and Robert nervously watches as a travel lift raises his yawl's bottom into view for the first time. Worms, worms doing their dirty work, but only a few, and not very deep into the thick cedar strip planks of the hull. By checking papers left on the boat and making telephone calls to a previous long-term owner, we piece together the story of RAINBOW'S END, designed by Cyrus Hamlin of Maine and built in 1963 by the prestigious Goudy and Stevens Boatyard. She was well cared for until just a few years ago, when she began to suffer from neglect. Now Robert has the job of bringing her back to life, although he has no idea how expensive and time consuming that job will be.

We begin. The hull below the waterline is sandblasted, and wormy places routed out and replaced. As I strip paint off the transom, the layered previous names of the yawl are revealed, one after the other—WINGS OF THE MORNING, WANDERLUST, AUDACIOUS and finally, RAINBOW'S END. Robert renames her ALLIANCE, pronounced the French way, "al-e-awnce." It's going to take an alliance to fix her up, all right, but we all think she's worth fixing. In December, after hull repairs are complete, he and Charlie sail her back to Charleston.

The problem of too many boats is beginning to mess up my life. I'm drawing social security, eligible for Medicare and too old and poor to be doing all of this work on three boats. Mary and I agree we must simplify our boat lives. Either we give up VERTROUWEN and the life in France, or we sell MARY M. We can't keep rushing back and forth from boat to boat, fixing this and that, and never relaxing on one boat in one place. If the choice was only between boats, we'd probably have to choose MARY M, a more spacious and comfortable boat. But, it's also a choice of destinations, what we're going to see and how far we have to go to see it. For the convenience of enjoying a variety of beautiful and interesting destinations we have to choose the unlimited possibilities in France and the rest of Europe over any boat accessible area of the United States we know of. Also, now that we own a piece of ALLIANCE, we're due lots of sailing trips to pay back our efforts and expenses. As I scrape latex paint and wallpaper off of rotted bulkheads, I often think of that missionary's vision. We decide to try one more season of cruising on both boats. We'll go to France early, cruise VERTROUWEN to Nancy, via Rheims and the World War I battlefields near Verdun, and return to South Carolina in time to cruise MARY M up the ICW to Maine.

MARY M's main salon

Each year I try to find the least expensive round trip flight from Charleston to Paris. This winter, a friend recommends a travel agent in Seattle with low fare tickets, so I call her and buy tickets to Paris, via Detroit. On April 10 we leave on time from Charleston. We have a 3 hour layover in Detroit, and the Paris flight is 2 additional hours late in leaving. Six hours into the flight, the pilot tells us they had radio trouble, started to turn back to Detroit, then followed another European bound flight toward Paris, but don't have enough fuel to get to Paris. The plane has to land in Ireland to refuel. Finally, we land at DeGaulle, 7 hours late, maybe in time to catch the day's final TGV train to Dijon. The last piece of our baggage rolls out onto the carousel, we pile it onto a cart with a broken wheel and start toward the train station, which is on a different level but inside the air terminal. In front of a crowded elevator Mary is being helped by a friendly woman who holds the door open, while I maneuver the baggage cart. The friendly woman steps back from the door and it closes, as Mary suddenly realizes the friendly woman has stolen the wallet out of her pocketbook. The elevator descends, the door opens and there's no policeman in sight. We know, from all the stories we've heard, that there's nothing we can do but go on our way. Mary's lost her passport, credit cards and French francs. I find a foreign currency exchange booth and trade all of my dollars for francs, getting a lousy exchange rate. Mary finds the train ticket counter and buys tickets to Dijon. We're hunting for the train, when an official tells Mary there's a strike, and the only train to Dijon leaves from a station in the center of Paris. Mary changes the tickets and we rush to find a taxi stand. The taxi driver knows the time of the last train to Dijon and says he might be able to make it. It's the most harrowing taxi ride in memory, even surpassing rides in Greece and Saudi Arabia. He pulls into the station 2 minutes before the train is supposed to leave. A porter hurries us through a gate and up a passageway between the trains, throwing our baggage onto a car, just as it starts to move. The train is jammed with passengers and we have to sit on jump seats between the cars for 2 hours. When we arrive in Dijon, the last local train to St Jean de Losne has already left and all of the rental car agencies are closed. Mary stays with the baggage while I find a hotel. We schlep the baggage a block to a nice little hotel and up to our room. This is our all time worst trip, 24 hours from Belle Isle to Dijon, plus a stolen wallet.

We're finally back on VERTROUWEN, admiring the new varnish job on her wood trim, for which we had to pay an enormous amount, even split three ways. It's cold and wet this spring, and melting snow from the mountains has the Saone River running fast. We delay our start up the Saone for 2 weeks, and are glad we have only a short slog before turning off, into the

Canal de la Marne. We rush along, through the continuing cold rain and sleet of April, make all of our prearranged rendezvous with friends, take a day's train detour to the American embassy in Paris for a new passport, arrive in Nancy 5 weeks later, turn VERTROUWEN over to our partners and fly home to board MARY M.

MARY M needs some work before we can start north, and it's hot in July before we finally get started. The snowbirds have long since arrived at their northern destinations. We hurry northward to the Chesapeake, still less than half way to Maine. Resting in a marina off the York River in Virginia, I get a telephone call from Robert, who says he's driving up to see us, with important news. Two days later, he and Molly, Leigh's younger sister, arrive to tell us they were married yesterday. They plan to live on ALLIANCE, as soon as she's ready.

We're pleased to have our sons married to two beautiful sisters, but we know they face many problems trying to make their cruising dreams come true. All of our sons are struggling in a world that's much more difficult and complicated than ours was. We planted the seed of escape in their minds and now we feel obligated to help them succeed. We taught them the joys of cruising but, apparently, we didn't stress that they had to make some money first. They're learning that now. At the end of the summer we list MARY M with a yacht broker in the Chesapeake and drive home.

Mary and I are comfortable in our snug Belle Isle place. Outside our door are two magnificent live oak trees and, by walking a few steps we can see the 1810 lighthouse at the mouth of Winyah Bay and watch boats cruise up and down the ICW. Inside, we're surrounded by our mementos, collected during 30 years of cruising. Mary's photographs and Charlie's paintings cover the walls. The boys still like to meet at Belle Isle occasionally, to work on Robert's sailboat and reminisce about the place their cruising lives began. I'm sitting in front of a fire in the fireplace, reading Kenneth Grahame's The Wind in the Willows, Chapter 9, "Wayfarers All", the part where an old Sea Rat tries to talk young Ratty into leaving his home and joining him:

"...and you, you will come too, young brother; for the days pass, and never return, and the south still waits for you, a blithsome step forward, and you are out of the old life and into the new! Then, some day long hence, jog home here if you will, when the cup has been drained and the play has been played, and sit down by your quiet river with a store of goodly memories for company. You can easily overtake me on the road, for you are young, and I am aging and go softly. I will linger and look back; and at last I will surely see you coming, eager and light hearted, with all the south in your face!"

Edmund is born to Molly and Robert on March 4, 2002. Leigh and Jamie are expecting a third in November. We worry about our family's problems and support their dreams, but each spring we'll leave them behind and return to VERTROUWEN, now approaching her 100th birthday, and continue to cruise the canals of Europe.

Sunflower at VERTROUWEN's porthole